Chess Explained:
The c3 Sicilian

Sam Collins

First published in the UK by Gambit Publications Ltd 2007

ISBN-13: 978-1-904600-71-8
ISBN-10: 1-904600-71-9

DISTRIBUTION:
Worldwide (except USA): Central Books Ltd, 99 Wallis Rd, London E9 5LN, England.
Tel +44 (0)20 8986 4854 Fax +44 (0)20 8533 5821. E-mail: orders@Centralbooks.com

Gambit Publications Ltd, 99 Wallis Rd, London E9 5LN, England.
E-mail: info@gambitbooks.com
Website (regularly updated): www.gambitbooks.com

Edited by Graham Burgess
Typeset by John Nunn
Cover image by Wolff Morrow
Printed in Great Britain by The Cromwell Press, Trowbridge, Wilts.

10 9 8 7 6 5 4 3 2 1

Gambit Publications Ltd
Managing Director: Murray Chandler GM
Chess Director: Dr John Nunn GM
Editorial Director: Graham Burgess FM
German Editor: Petra Nunn WFM
Webmaster: Dr Helen Milligan WFM

Contents

Symbols

+	check
++	double check
#	checkmate
!!	brilliant move
!	good move
!?	interesting move
?!	dubious move
?	bad move
??	blunder
Ch	championship
1-0	the game ends in a win for White
½-½	the game ends in a draw
0-1	the game ends in a win for Black
(D)	see next diagram

Bibliography

Books
Collins, *An Attacking Repertoire for White* (Batsford 2004)
Collins, *Understanding the Chess Openings* (Gambit 2005)
Nunn, *Understanding Chess Move by Move* (Gambit 2002)
Rogozenko, *Anti-Sicilians: A Guide for Black* (Gambit 2003)
Rozentalis and Harley, *Play the 2 c3 Sicilian* (Gambit 2002)

Databases
ChessBase Mega Database 2006

Periodicals
New In Chess Yearbook

Websites
Chess Publishing (www.chesspublishing.com)
The Week in Chess (www.chesscenter.com/twic/twic.html)

Introduction

The Chess Explained series seeks to provide the reader with a basic understanding of an opening line through the use of 25 games, annotated with relatively few variations but plenty of verbal commentary. I think the c3 Sicilian is a pretty good candidate for such a format, for two reasons:

1) There is less theory than in, say, the Najdorf Sicilian or Grünfeld. In extremely sharp openings, the assessment of many positions depends critically on specific and often complex variations. The opening in this text, however, lends itself to verbal explanation because the positions are inherently more rational than in those sharper lines.

2) There is quite a lot of thematic overlap between individual variations – positions with an isolated queen's pawn or e5-spearhead, for instance, come up extremely frequently, and knowledge is readily transferable from one line to the next.

Why Play the c3 Sicilian?

I've never been a fan of negative campaigning, but I'm going to indulge in a little here. Some facts about the Open Sicilian:

1) White has never, ever, shown a clear route to an advantage.

2) Learning and maintaining a complete repertoire as White in the Open Sicilian requires the single largest time investment of any chess project.

Turning the merits of our candidate:

1) The main reason people play the c3 Sicilian is because it doesn't take much time to learn, and maintaining one's knowledge is simpler because the theory develops fairly slowly. Also, developments don't in general dramatically alter existing assessments, so the price of not knowing a new move will normally be pretty minimal.

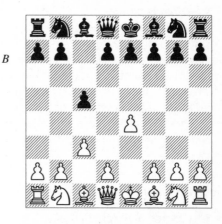

B

2) Some, like Tiviakov, maintain that the c3 Sicilian gives better chances of an advantage than the Open Sicilian. This argument needs to be broken down a little:

2a) On an objective basis (i.e. assuming best play from both sides), the c3 Sicilian doesn't give White more chances of an advantage than an Open Sicilian. Sorry.

2b) On a subjective basis, I think the c3 Sicilian gives some extra chances of an edge, since Sicilian players inevitably devote more time and effort to learning the lines after 2 ♘f3 and 3 d4, so they often don't know the best responses to the c3 lines.

Common Criticisms of the c3 Sicilian

Most of these are articulated by Sicilian players, who have a vested interest in encouraging more Open Sicilians. For instance, Garry Kasparov's criticism of 2 ♘f3 d6 3 ♗b5+ was motivated in no small part by the fact that his results in that line were worse than after 3 d4. Incidentally, the great man has opted for the c3 Sicilian on 12 occasions, though most of these games are from simuls. Needless to say, he made an immense score with White in those games.

The c3 Sicilian gives no advantage

Fine, but nor does the Open Sicilian. The subjective/objective distinction, outlined above, holds true here – clearly White can't win the game with best play, but he gets an edge from the opening more often than Black does.

The c3 Sicilian is boring

This one has a little more foundation. Certainly, the positions arising in this book are generally less complicated than in the Najdorf or Sveshnikov. Several of the main lines result in endgames, which are not to everyone's taste. That said, White has some decent attacking chances in many lines, especially those where he obtains an isolated queen's pawn (IQP) or related structure.

A Note on Move-Orders

After 1 e4 c5, the only certain way to get the positions arising in this book is to play 2 c3. However, many of the games herein open 1 e4 c5 2 ♘f3, and only after 2...♘c6 or 2...e6 does White play 3 c3.

The good news about the 2 ♘f3 move-order is that both 2...e6 and 2...♘c6 significantly cut down on Black's options – the former obviously precludes any systems based on ...♗g4 (or ...g6, which wouldn't sit well with ...e6), while the latter spends a move developing a knight which is not involved in the early stages of several major systems (for instance, Black no longer has the option, after 1 e4 c5 2 c3 d5 3 exd5 ♕xd5 4 d4 ♘f6 5 ♘f3, of 5...♗g4 or 5...e6, each of which is more popular than 5...♘c6). In contrast, White loses very little by

putting his knight on f3, since it goes here very early in every system with the exception of some harmless sidelines. The bad news is that, after 1 e4 c5 2 ♘f3, Black can play 2...d6, after which White can play an Open Sicilian with 3 d4 or an interesting sideline with 3 c3, but there is no path to the variations covered herein.

The 2 ♘f3 move-order is used by c3 Sicilian players in two instances:

1) If they are happy with the position after 1 e4 c5 2 ♘f3 d6 – this could be because they occasionally play the Open Sicilian, or know something about the 3 c3 line;

2) If they know that their opponent won't play 2...d6. This happens quite often, since only Najdorf, Dragon, Classical and Scheveningen players can use a 2...d6 move-order.

The Format

I considered including preliminary structural diagrams in the chapter introductions. However, while I often find these worthwhile, I opted instead to discuss structural issues more fully in the concrete and practical context of the games themselves. However, I have penned brief chapter introductions so that the reader can get an idea of how the various lines fit together.

As to suggested repertoires, the game conclusions indicate all of my preferences.

As always, my deepest thanks go to my friends and family, my publishing team, and my readers. I welcome all comments concerning the material contained herein, and these can be addressed to samcollins@bcmchess.co.uk

Sam Collins
London, January 2007

1 2...♞f6: Lines with cxd4

1 e4 c5 2 c3 ♞f6

This is one of Black's two main defences, the other being 2...d5. Both Tiviakov and Sveshnikov (noted experts on the c3 Sicilian) believe that 2...♞f6 is Black's best defence. Now White can't defend with 3 ♞c3, since this square is occupied by a pawn. While pushing his e-pawn gains time on the knight, this is at the cost of leaving a comfortable square for the horse on d5 – White will be reluctant to move his c-pawn again to kick this piece, especially since Black already has some pawn-control over the important d4-square.

3 e5

Much as in the Alekhine Defence, this move is a gift and a curse. White gains time and space at the cost of weakening his central control. In particular, he can't obtain a two-abreast pawn-centre any more.

3...♞d5

No prizes for other moves.

4 d4

This is White's most direct approach. Even though he can't get his perfect centre any more, there are benefits to having a pawn on d4. It holds the e5-pawn and, by encouraging an exchange, frees the c3-square.

4...cxd4

In practice, this is pretty automatic. Other moves give White the opportunity to chase the knight with c4 and d5.

5 ♞f3

Even if White is planning to recapture on d4 with a pawn, it's advisable to throw this move in.

5...e6

By defending the knight, Black threatens to capture the c3-pawn. On the other hand, he has ruled out possibilities of developing his queen's bishop to g4. Sometimes these ...e6 lines are regarded as inferior by specialists like Sveshnikov and Tiviakov, but I don't see any theoretical or practical basis for this view.

5...♞c6 keeps Black's options open – he might try to develop the light-squared bishop to g4, or develop his king's bishop to g7, or just transpose into ...e6 systems. White also has some options since the d4-pawn is still pinned – in particular, the theory of 6 ♗c4 has been extensively developed and will be examined in Chapter 2. However, he can also simply take: 6 cxd4 was White's choice in Game 1, Pavasović-Halkias.

6 cxd4

Now that Black has committed himself and locked in his light-squared bishop, White makes the natural recapture. It's arguable whether he can let Black take on c3, but this would definitely be a sacrifice.

6...d6

Hitting the e5-pawn, while freeing the d7-square for either a knight or a bishop.

6...b6 is a major alternative, preparing to move the bishop to b7 or a6. Game 5, Khairullin-S.Novikov, covers this.

7 ♗c4

Putting the bishop on an aggressive square and preparing to castle.

7 a3 is the big alternative, preparing ♗d3 without allowing the annoying ...♘b4. This is examined in Game 4, Marković-Rublevsky.

Now (after 7 ♗c4):

7...♘c6 develops and puts pressure on the e5-pawn. Game 2, Mamedyarov-Ramirez, covers this plan.

7...♘b6 is the alternative, planning an interesting idea: ...dxe5 and ...♘c6!?, which leads to unbalanced IQP positions. Have a look at Game 3, Stević-Mastrovasilis.

Game 1
Duško Pavasović – Stelios Halkias
Vidmar Memorial, Terme Zrece 2003

1 e4 c5 2 c3 ♘f6 3 e5 ♘d5 4 d4 cxd4 5 ♘f3 *(D)*

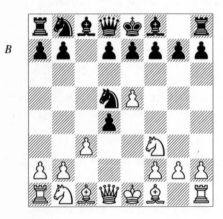

B

5...♘c6

5...d6 6 ♕xd4 is also an important line: after 6...e6 7 exd6 ♕xd6 8 ♗d3 ♘c6 9 ♕e4 ♗e7 10 0-0 White has some advantage since Black's pieces are less active, while White's play is automatic – move a rook to the d-file, the queen's knight to d2 (and probably e4) and see what Black does.

6 cxd4 d6

Hitting the e5-pawn and preparing ...♗g4.

7 ♗c4

The knight is attacked, and Black can either retreat it or protect it.

7 ♗d2!? is an offbeat idea, preparing to develop the knight to c3 now that the bishop can recapture. Its main virtue is that it avoids the theory inherent in 7 ♗c4. Its main problem is that it is virtually unthinkable that White can achieve any advantage after such a move.

7...♘b6

Tarrasch was famously critical of placing knights on b6 (or b3), and this odd dictum certainly applies here. The knight, apart from controlling a couple of light squares, serves a limited function and is quite difficult to relocate. In the game, White's pawn sacrifice is based in large part on this piece, which has a hard time pulling its weight.

7...e6 transposes to the 5...e6 6 cxd4 d6 7 ♗c4 ♘c6 line – see Game 2.

7...dxe5 leads to interesting play. White can take on e5 with either the pawn or the knight, but the main theoretical argument has revolved around Kaidanov's committal 8 ♗xd5 ♕xd5 9 ♘c3, when Black is in some danger of getting crushed. However, if he makes it to the middlegame, his long-term chances should be favourable. The main, and most contentious, lines occur after 9...♕d6 10 d5 ♘d4 11 ♘xd4 exd4 12 ♕xd4 e5 13 ♕d3 ♗d7 14 0-0 f5!?, when Black will follow up with ...♔f7 and ...e4, while White will try to attack the king by bringing the rooks to the centre, his bishop to b2 and his queen to the kingside.

We now return to 7...♘b6 *(D)*:

8 ♗b3!?

This is a line with some bite. Scottish GM John Shaw mentioned this bishop retreat to me some years ago, and it's definitely much more interesting than 8 ♗b5. Black's defence isn't too easy, whatever theory says.

8 ♗b5 dxe5 9 ♘xe5 ♗d7 doesn't give White anything. This dull position has been tested in hundreds of games. A typical line now runs 10

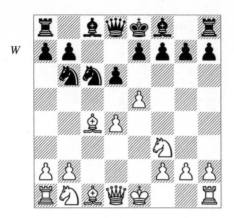

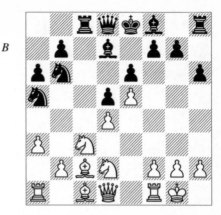

♗xc6 ♗xc6 11 ♘xc6 bxc6 12 0-0 g6 13 ♖e1 ♗g7 14 ♗g5. This looks dangerous, but there's an easy tactical solution: 14...0-0! 15 ♗xe7 ♕xd4 16 ♕xd4 ♗xd4 17 ♘d2 and Black moves his f8-rook, with an extremely drawish ending.

8...dxe5

This is critical. The main defect of White's 8th move was that it left the c6-knight unpinned, which increases Black's control over the centre and means that White can't recapture on e5 without allowing a queen exchange on d1. While there are several endgames where White can fight for an advantage after such an exchange, this isn't one of them.

8...d5 is a tricky move, since White's best is the unlikely move 9 ♘h4!, preventing the light-squared bishop from developing to either f5 or g4. White then has a pretty good French. Collins-Dominguez Aguilar, Turin Olympiad 2006 proceeded 9...e6 10 ♘f3 (it's also possible to play 10 g3 ♗e7 11 ♕g4, but as an Advance French player I was perfectly happy with the simple knight retreat, because I now have a very comfortable and simple development plan which simply can't be played in the French; also, as before, I don't like the knight on b6) 10...♗d7 11 ♘c3 (it's important to cover the b5-square in order to prevent ...♘a5 and ...♗b5) 11...♖c8 12 0-0 (it is also possible to play 12 ♗g5, when Black is pretty much compelled to respond with 12...f6 since the exchange of dark-squared bishops is very unfavourable for him) 12...h6 13 a3 (it's useful to take control of the b4-square, since now White can play ♗c2 and ♕d3) 13...a6 14 ♗c2 ♘a5 15 ♘d2 (D).

Black is now in major trouble; White has a bunch of useful moves (♕g4, ♗d3, ♘e2-f4-h5) while Black has no play and won't be able to castle for ages. My opponent decided on a risky plan of advancing on the kingside: 15...g6?! (it was better to wait for f4 before playing this, since now my dark-squared bishop has access to the kingside) 16 ♗d3 h5 17 ♕f3 ♗h6 18 ♕g3 h4?! (18...♕g5? loses to 19 ♘de4 ♕xg3 20 ♘d6+ and 21 fxg3, but this just weakens the kingside) 19 ♕g4 ♕g5 20 ♕h3 ♕e7 21 ♘f3 ♘b3 22 ♗xh6 ♖xh6 23 ♖ad1 ♔f8 24 ♘d2. White's play is extremely simple – all exchanges favour him, since they just accentuate the weakness of Black's light-squared bishop. Alex Baburin once explained this concept to me with an ice hockey analogy – if one player is sent off, a 5 vs 4 advantage is useful, a 4 vs 3 advantage is much larger, and a 3 vs 2 advantage is decisive. A similar logic can be used when playing against a bad piece – the more pieces which leave the board, the more Black will rely on his useless bishop. After 24...♘xd2 (Black couldn't play 24...♘xd4 in view of 25 ♕e3) 25 ♖xd2 ♔g7 26 ♖c2 ♖hh8 27 ♖fc1 ♕g5 28 ♕e3 ♕e7 (exchanging on e3 would just strengthen the d4-pawn, give White the half-open f-file to work with, and introduce the possibility of an e4 break) 29 h3 ♖c7 30 ♘e2 ♖xc2 31 ♖xc2 ♖c8 32 ♖xc8 ♘xc8 33 ♕c1 ♕d8 34 ♔h2! followed by ♘g1-f3 and ♕f4 White had a perfect position.

9 d5! (D)

This is the key move – the dull endgames arising from a capture on e5 promise nothing for White.

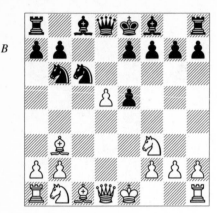

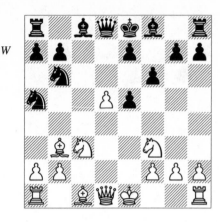

9...♘a5

With this move, Black manages to exchange off White's light-squared bishop, which is a definite achievement.

No other knight moves can be recommended here. 9...♘b4 10 ♘c3 e6 seems like a logical continuation, but 11 ♗g5! gives White a very dangerous initiative. Pavasović-Kurnosov, European Ch, Istanbul 2003 continued 11...f6 12 ♘xe5!!. The objective consequences of this move aren't completely clear-cut, but Black has an extremely difficult defensive task in practical terms since his king has to take a walk. I wonder how much of what follows was on Pavasović's laptop before the game. 12...fxg5 13 ♕h5+ g6 (13...♔e7? is met by the superb 14 ♘e4!!, when Black can resign) 14 ♘xg6 hxg6 15 ♕xh8 ♘d3+ 16 ♔f1 exd5 17 ♕d4 ♘f4 18 h4! (undermining the knight and getting the h1-rook into the game; Black has two pieces for a rook, but his queenside is undeveloped and he'll have a hard time getting his king to safety) 18...♗e6? 19 ♖e1 ♕c7 20 hxg5 0-0-0 21 ♖h4! (the winning move – White can even afford to 'sacrifice' the exchange on f4, since the e6-bishop will fall next) 21...♗f5 22 ♕xf4 ♗d6 23 ♕d2 ♗c5 24 ♘b5 ♘c4 25 ♗xc4 dxc4 26 ♖e8 ♕b6 27 ♘xa7+ 1-0.

10 ♘c3

Holding the d5-pawn while continuing development.

10...♘xb3

This knight cannot do anything more useful.

10...f6!? *(D)* was chosen in Pavasović-Gelfand, Vidmar Memorial, Portorož 2001.

The Israeli GM is famed for this thorough preparation, and this line could really catch on. 11 0-0 g6 (this is the point – the bishop can develop to g7, and Black either hides his king on f7 or castles, in either case bringing his rook into the game) 12 ♗e3 ♗g7 13 ♗c5 ♗g4 (castling wouldn't have been too smart) 14 h3 ♗xf3 15 ♕xf3 ♘xb3 16 axb3 0-0 (now this is a safe move for Black to make, since there won't be any accidents on the a2-g8 diagonal) 17 ♖fd1 ♕d7 18 d6 exd6 and a draw was agreed, though I think White has an edge after 19 ♗xd6, because both ♗xf8 and ♗xe5 are threatened and, when he regains his material, White will have the more active game. Incidentally, there was no value in 18...e6, since apart from being able to regain the pawn with 19 ♗xb6 and 20 ♘a4, White clearly has enormous compensation for the pawn due to his monster passed pawn on d6.

11 ♕xb3

By recapturing in this fashion, White develops and introduces the idea of ♕b5+. which is a crucial resource in the main line.

The pseudo-active 11 axb3?!, aiming to generate play down the a-file, leaves Black very comfortable after 11...e6.

11...e6

This isn't Black's only option, but remains his most popular one.

12 ♘xe5 *(D)*

Temporarily regaining the pawn and bringing the knight to a more active square.

12...exd5

Again the most popular, but not necessarily the best.

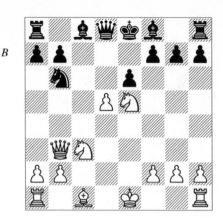

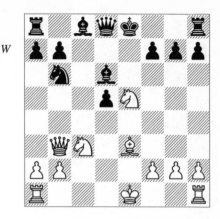

12...♘xd5 has been tried by a few strong players, with quite reasonable results. Black relies on tactics to simplify the position (you can see in the main game how awkwardly placed the knight can be on b6). Rogozenko commented that this move of Tregubov's might be an easier way to solve Black's problems than the move in our main game. Then 13 ♕b5+ ♗d7 14 ♕xb7 ♗b4 leads to an interesting position. Fressinet opted for 15 ♗d2, which is OK, but 15 ♘xd7!? forces Black to walk a tightrope. Then 15...♕c8 is the only move, when the main line of my analysis runs 16 ♘c5!! (blocking the c-file) 16...♕xb7 17 ♘xb7 ♖b8 18 ♗d2 ♖xb7 19 ♘xd5 exd5 20 0-0-0 with a good endgame for White.

12...♗d6 is also a move. After 13 ♕b5+ ♔f8 14 dxe6 ♗xe6 15 ♗f4 Black still has problems with his h8-rook. He doesn't have an extra pawn to compensate, but rather relies on the activity of his developed pieces. After 15...♘c4! White can choose 16 0-0-0 with a complicated game, or play 16 ♘xc4 ♗xf4 17 ♘e3 ♕d7 18 ♕b4+ ♗d6 19 ♕d4, when the two bishops could prove effective in the long term, but I'd take White since the h8-rook is still a major problem.

13 ♗e3!

It's more important to attack the knight than to castle.

13...♗d6 (D)

Developing with gain of time.

14 ♕b5+!

The only move. After 14 ♘f3 0-0 White has an uphill struggle to draw, since lines where he takes on b6 and d5 will leave Black with two dominant bishops.

14...♔f8!

I don't know who'd work out that this is the best move unless they knew the theory. In any event, White's compensation is now pretty obvious – just look at the h8-rook, coupled with Black's underdevelopment.

14...♗d7 15 ♘xd7 ♕xd7 16 0-0-0! leaves White with a huge initiative since all of his pieces are rushing into play while the black rooks are napping. In Pavasović-Panchenko, Pula 2001 Black resigned after 16...♕xb5 17 ♘xb5 ♔d7 18 ♗xb6 axb6 19 ♖xd5 ♔c6 20 ♖hd1 ♗c5 21 ♘c3 ♖he8 22 a3 ♖e6 23 ♔c2 since White had a decisive threat of 24 b4.

15 ♘f3

Now this is the most appropriate.

15 0-0-0 is sharper, but I think White is compromising his king safety too much. After 15...♗e6 Black is ready to play down the c-file.

15...♗d7

By driving the queen back to b3, Black forces White to play ♘d4. This reduces his chances of regaining the pawn in the near-future, but also establishes a useful bind which, in my opinion, more than compensates for the material deficit.

15...♗e6 16 0-0 ♘c4 (D) is Rogozenko's recommendation.

I've done some analysis on this position, and think that White can retain some advantage: 17 ♕xb7 ♕c8 18 ♕xc8+ ♖xc8 19 ♗d4 ♗c5 (19...a6 20 b3 ♘a5 21 ♘a4 ♘c6 is given as equal by Rozentalis and Harley but 22 ♗c5!

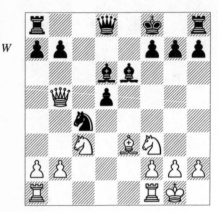

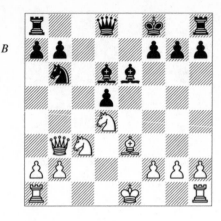

looks quite pleasant for White) and now the main line has been 20 ♗xc5+ ♖xc5 21 ♘a4 ♖c8 22 b3 ♘a3 23 ♘d4 ♔e7 24 ♖ac1 ♔d6, which left White slightly better in Pavasović-Jelen, Ljubljana 2002, but I recommend 20 ♖ac1 ♔e7 21 b3!? (Rogozenko only considered 21 ♗xg7) 21...♗xd4 22 ♘xd4 ♘b2 (22...♘e5 23 ♖fd1 is also a little better for White) 23 ♘ce2 ♘d3 24 ♖cd1 ♘c5 25 ♖fe1 with an edge for White – the d-pawn is solidly blockaded, the black bishop is passive and the white position looks more active.

16 ♕b3

Bringing the queen back to its best square, where it monitors both the d5- and b7-pawns.

16...♗e6

This is the logical follow-up. 16...♗c6 takes care of the weak pawns on the b- and d-files, but at the cost of putting the bishop on a horrible square. An indicative continuation might be 17 0-0 ♘c4 18 ♗d4!? followed by ♖fe1 with good compensation.

17 ♘d4 (D)

The d-pawn is now solidly blockaded, and is restricting both the b6-knight and the e6-bishop.

17...♔g8

17...♘c4 is a more aggressive treatment, when I think White is best advised to decline the b-pawn and simply play 18 0-0!. Black will be reluctant to open the f-file with ...♘xe3.

18 0-0

A much cosier domestic arrangement than that experienced by the black king – the h8-rook just can't get into play.

18...♖c8

A logical move, but it doesn't do much to upset White.

19 ♖fe1

White has excellent compensation for his pawn. Black sorely needs the h8-rook to defend the centre and the queenside, but it's firmly locked out of play.

19...♕d7 20 ♘cb5!

The correct knight to put on b5 – now White pressurizes all three black minor pieces.

20...♗b8

White has enormous pressure, and Pavasović cashes in:

21 ♘xe6 ♕xe6

21...fxe6 leaves White with several tempting options – as well as regaining his pawn with 22 ♘xa7 ♗xa7 23 ♗xb6, he can retain the pressure with 22 ♗xb6 axb6 23 ♕h3, when he has excellent compensation since Black's light squares are collapsing.

22 ♗xb6

The black queen is forced away from the defence of the d5-pawn.

22...♕xb6 23 ♕xd5 (D)

White has retained his advantage in piece activity (indeed, it has increased) while regaining his pawn. To avoid immediate disaster, Halkias decides to exchange queens, but the endgame is also superb for White.

23...♕c6 24 ♕xc6 bxc6

Forced because of the weakness of Black's back rank.

25 ♖ac1 g6

The king has to get off the back rank – there was an immediate threat of 26 ♖xc6.

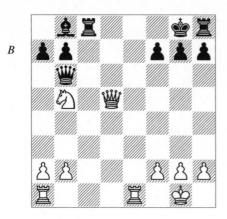

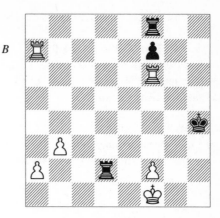

26 ♖e7!

Rook to the seventh rank is an automatic move. The a7-pawn is now doomed.

26...♔g7 27 ♘xa7 ♗xa7

Otherwise Black would drop another pawn.

28 ♖xa7 ♖he8

Trying to gain some activity, but Pavasović deals with it astutely.

29 ♔f1 ♖cd8 30 ♖e1!

Just in time to cover the weaknesses on the second rank.

30...♖f8 31 g3 ♖d2 32 ♖e2 ♖fd8 33 ♖ee7!

The position with two rooks might be winning for White, but with four rooks it's even better.

33...♖f8 34 b3

White has total domination as well as extra material.

34...♔h6 35 h4!

Restricting the black king to a square where it runs a serious risk of getting mated.

35...g5

Black makes a desperate attempt at activity.

36 hxg5+ ♔xg5 37 ♖ec7

Taking on f7 was also possible, but this way White doesn't even lose his a2-pawn.

37...h5

Black desperately tries to liquidate some pawns on the kingside, but it's not enough.

38 ♖xc6

Now the tally is increased to two pawns.

38...h4 39 gxh4+ ♔xh4 40 ♖f6! *(D)*

Cutting off the king and performing some important defence and offence on the f-file.

40...♔g5 41 ♖fxf7

White could retain more pawns with 41 ♖f3, but there's no real cause for this. The endgame with two extra pawns is trivial, though still requiring attention – in the Kasparov-Short match of 1993, Kasparov allowed (and Short missed!) a drawing resource in a similar endgame. One of the advantages White has over that position, however, is that the black king is cut off.

41...♖xf7 42 ♖xf7 ♖xa2 43 ♖f3

Pavasović's technique is up to the task.

43...♖b2 44 ♖d3 ♔f4 45 f3

This might look odd, since now the white king is temporarily cut off. However, the white pawns and rook are in a mutually protective formation, and Pavasović's winning plan is very convincing.

45...♖a2 46 ♔e1 ♔e5 47 ♔d1 ♖b2 48 ♔c1 ♖h2 49 ♔b1 ♔e6 50 b4!

Now the white rook can occupy the perfect position – behind the b-pawn while supporting the f-pawn.

50...♖h4 51 ♖b3 ♔d6 52 b5 ♔c7 53 ♔c2 ♖d4 54 ♔c3 ♖d6 55 b6+ ♔b7

Naturally, if Black takes the pawn, the white king easily reaches a decisive square on the kingside before advancing his pawn: 55...♖xb6 56 ♖xb6 ♔xb6 57 ♔d4 ♔c6 58 ♔e5 ♔d7 59 ♔f6 followed by queening.

56 ♔c4 ♖d1 57 ♔c5 ♖d2 58 f4! ♖f2 59 ♖b4

White has pushed most of his position up one rank, which increases his chances of sacrificing the b-pawn and running with his f-pawn.

59...♖d2 60 ♖d4 ♖c2+ 61 ♔d6 ♔xb6 62 ♖b4+!

Not strictly necessary, but a helpful finesse anyway.

62...♔a5 63 ♖b8 ♖f2 64 ♔e5 1-0

This position is winning when the black king is cut off by one file. When he's cut off by four, it's definitely time to resign.

Conclusions

1) I think the main lines, where Black accepts the pawn sacrifice, are pretty attractive for White. He gets a lot of compensation if Black tries to keep the pawn. Black's best approaches involve trying to return the pawn in order to simplify the position, but even here White has some chances of retaining an edge.

2) Gelfand's idea at move 10 is noteworthy, and would probably be my choice with Black. White needs to find something in order to claim a workable edge here.

3) 8 ♗b5 is boring and not very good.

Game 2
Shakhriyar Mamedyarov – Alejandro Ramirez Alvarez
Wijk aan Zee 2005

1 e4 c5 2 c3 ♘f6 3 e5 ♘d5 4 ♘f3 d6 *(D)*

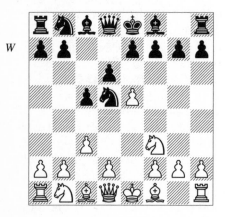

This is a tricky move-order. In the game, we transpose to a main line which can be reached via several routes, but it's important to be aware of the deviations.

5 ♗c4

5 exd6 ♕xd6 6 d4 cxd4 7 ♘xd4 reminds me a little of a Tarrasch French. After 7...a6 8 ♘d2 g6 9 ♘c4 ♕d8 10 a4, White had some advantage in Vogt-Cvitan, Swiss Team Ch 1999.

5 ♘a3 is an interesting independent alternative. I'm not completely sure what's going on here, since there haven't been any high-level encounters in this position.

5 d4 is possible, of course, but in some ways this gives Black what he wants since White has lost the flexibility inherent in 4 ♘f3, without

getting a 'concession' like ...e6. While I'm not completely comfortable with this assessment of ...e6 lines as inferior to other stuff, it's certain that once Black plays ...e6 White has few options other than d4, whereas White can experiment with delaying d4 against other lines.

5...e6

5...♘b6 *(D)* leads to interesting play. White has a couple of very sharp tries, but they don't seem to lead anywhere:

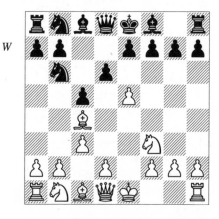

a) Golod analyses 6 ♗xf7+? ♔xf7 7 ♘g5+ ♔g8 8 ♕f3 ♕e8 9 e6 g6, when Black is winning.

b) 6 e6!? is an enterprising attempt, but Stević-Palac, Croatian Ch, Pula 2000 demonstrated a good antidote: 6...♘xc4 7 ♕a4+ ♘c6 8 exf7+ ♔xf7 9 ♕xc4+ d5! 10 ♕xc5 e5 and the central domination provides interesting compensation for Black.

c) After 6 ♗b3 c4 7 ♗c2 Black can transpose into a main line with 7...♘c6, or keep play in independent channels with 7...dxe5 8 ♘xe5. In this position, the strong theoretician Bogdan Lalić risked 8...♕d5 against Sermek at Šibenik 2005, but the c3 Sicilian specialist responded accurately: 9 ♕e2! ♕xg2 10 ♗e4 ♕g5 11 ♘xc4 e6 12 ♘ba3 ♕d8 13 d4 ♘xc4 14 ♘xc4 ♘d7 15 ♗f4 ♘f6 16 ♗f3 ♗e7 17 0-0-0 0-0 18 ♖hg1 with an absolutely perfect position for White. Black can try the more conservative 8...♘8d7 instead, with the aim of simplifying the position.

6 0-0 ♘c6 7 d4 cxd4

It's rarely in Black's interest to refrain from capturing on d4. For instance, 7...dxe5 8 dxe5 favours White – he can build up naturally behind the e-pawn (♘bd2-e4, ♕e2) and while the white c-pawn usefully guards both b4 and d4, the black c-pawn seems to be something of a target.

8 cxd4 ♗e7 *(D)*

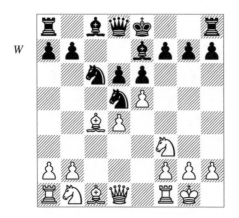

This position can be reached via a bunch of move-orders – for instance, 4 d4 cxd4 5 ♘f3 e6 6 cxd4 d6 7 ♗c4 ♘c6 8 0-0 ♗e7.

9 ♕e2

The queen prepares to occupy the e4-square, while leaving d1 open for a rook.

9 ♖e1 is a major alternative, and would be my principal recommendation to White. 9...0-0 10 exd6 ♕xd6 11 ♘c3 is the idea – White is angling for a good version of an IQP position.

Now 11...♘xc3 12 bxc3 b6 13 ♘g5! attacks the undefended kingside. I once played 13...g6, but after 14 h4! was in serious trouble. Black's best here is the uninspiring 13...♗xg5 14 ♗xg5 with an uphill struggle to contain the bishops. In Collins-Nokes, Turin Olympiad 2006, I managed to get the good side of this line. After 14...♗b7 15 ♕h5 ♘e7 16 ♗d3 ♘f5 17 ♕h3 ♕c6 18 ♖ad1 h6 I eventually managed to win after 19 ♗xf5, but simply 19 ♗f4 is even stronger, keeping ideas of ♗e5, and ♗xf5 followed by d5. Rogozenko suggests that Black shouldn't take on c3, and this seems a better attempt at equality: 11...♖d8 12 ♗b3 a6 13 ♕e2 b5, with reasonable chances.

The immediate 9 ♘c3 *(D)* is unpromising, since Black gets to exchange queens right away:

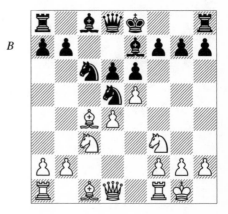

9...♘xc3 10 bxc3 dxe5 11 ♘xe5 (it's more sensible to take with the pawn, since ♘g5 can be a useful resource in the endgame; however, White has nothing there either) 11...♘xe5 12 dxe5 ♕xd1 13 ♖xd1 ♗d7 14 ♗e3 (White should play more actively with 14 a4) 14...♖c8 15 ♗e2 ♗c5 16 ♗d4 ♗xd4 17 ♖xd4 (taking with the pawn is even worse, since White's structure is still poor, but Black would also have a potential outside passed pawn) 17...♔e7 (capturing on c3 loses in a pretty basic way: 17...♖xc3?? 18 ♖ad1 ♖c7 19 ♖xd7! ♖xd7 20 ♗b5) 18 ♖ad1 ♖hd8 19 ♗f3 b6 20 c4 ♖c7! (a neat way to get out of the pin) 21 ♗e4 ♖dc8 22 ♗d3 ♖c5 23 f4 ♖8c7 with the better game for Black since he can play against the c-pawn and the a-pawn. In Harborne-Collins, Isle of Man

2002, I ended up doubling rooks on the a-file and winning material.

9...0-0

White now has to make two fundamental decisions:

1) Should he force the exchange of the d5-knight (rather than playing around it)?

2) Should he play exd6?

An example of White answering 'yes' to both questions is contained in the note to his 9th move. In the game, Mamedyarov opts for 'yes' to 1 and 'no' to 2. See the following note for a different way to handle the position.

10 ♘c3

10 ♕e4 (D) is the main line, or certainly was for a while.

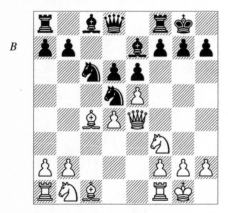

I feel well placed to discuss this here, since I have a terrible record with both colours! The first thing to appreciate is that, due to a combination of tactical and positional factors, White rarely threatens to win a pawn by capturing on d5, so Black should leave his knight in the middle. Thus:

a) Black can play 10...♕c7.

b) 10...♖e8 was given some harsh treatment in Motwani-Collins, British Ch, Edinburgh 2003: 11 ♖e1 (11 ♗xd5 exd5 12 ♕xd5 dxe5 13 ♕xd8 ♗xd8 14 dxe5 ♗g4 and Black regains his material with the better endgame) 11...♘b6 12 ♗d3 g6 13 ♘c3 ♘b4 14 ♗b1 ♘4d5 15 ♕g4 ♘xc3 16 bxc3 ♕c7 17 h4 ♘d7 (accepting the bait with 17...♕xc3 18 h5 is critical, but White has a very strong attack; Winants seemed to think it was a draw when he analysed the game

in *ChessBase Magazine*, but there are safer ways to draw with Black than this) 18 h5 f5 19 ♕g3 ♔g7 20 hxg6 hxg6. I knew my position was bad, but the next move still came as a shock: 21 ♗xf5!! exf5 22 exd6 ♗xd6 23 ♗h6+! (Paul is an extremely dangerous tactician, as is demonstrated to my cost in this game!) 23...♔xh6 24 ♕h4+ ♔g7 25 ♖xe8 ♘f8 26 ♖ae1 and I stopped the clocks in view of 27 ♖1e7+.

c) I think the simplest move is 10...♗d7. White has tried a variety of moves here, but I don't think they change the nature of the position. 11 ♖d1 ♖c8 was a position I had a couple of times with White, and only made one draw. 12 ♘bd2 (somehow I later forgot about this game and went for the ambitious 12 h4, but after 12...♘cb4 13 ♗b3 a5 14 a4 h6 15 ♗d2 dxe5 16 dxe5 ♕b6 17 ♘c3 ♗c5 18 ♖f1 f5! 19 exf6 ♘xf6 20 ♕g6 ♗e8 21 ♕b1 ♖d8 Black was doing very well in Collins-Bruno, European Team Ch, Gothenburg 2005) 12...♕b6 13 a3 ♕a5 14 ♗a2 ♕c7 15 ♘f1 ♘a5 16 ♘g5 ♕c2 17 exd6 ♗xg5 18 ♕xc2 ♖xc2 19 ♗xg5 ♖xb2 with equality in the endgame, Collins-Saevareid, Gausdal 2004.

10...♘xc3 11 bxc3 (D)

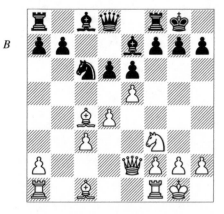

11...dxe5

This is a natural approach, slightly weakening the white pawns. It also avoids the type of isolated-pawn-couple structure which White obtained in the note to his 9th move.

11...d5? is a major strategic mistake, since after 12 ♗d3 there is no easy way to challenge White's kingside space advantage (...f6 would leave an ugly weakness on e6). It will be half a dozen moves before Black can even consider generating play against the c3-pawn, by which stage the white attack will be well advanced.

12 dxe5

12 ♘xe5 ♘xe5 13 dxe5 is worth looking into – I think White has chances of an edge here.

12...♕a5

This is an excellent square for the queen – it hits the e-pawn and has further options on c5 or a4.

13 ♕e4 ♕a4!

The pin looks pretty essential – otherwise ♗d3 would give White a very natural kingside build-up.

14 ♗g5 *(D)*

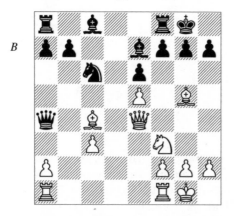

This provokes an exchange which has positive aspects for both players – White is getting rid of a bad bishop with few prospects (he'd love to put it on h6 after provoking ...g6, but there's no way to force this kingside concession) while Black is simplifying and making his spatial disadvantage less and less relevant.

14...h6

14...♗d7 15 ♖fd1 ♖ad8 was enough to draw after 16 ♗xe7 ♘xe7 17 ♕xb7 ♕xc4 in Pavasović-Sulava, Nova Gorica 1996. White should probably try 16 ♖ab1!? instead.

15 ♗xe7 ♘xe7

The c6-square is now available to the black bishop.

16 ♖ab1

This activates the white rook, though the restraint of the d7-bishop is purely cosmetic.

16 ♖fd1 is an interesting alternative: after 16...♗d7 (16...♖b8 17 ♖d4 ♕c6 18 ♗d3 ♕xe4 19 ♗xe4 b6 20 ♖a4 ♗b7 21 ♖xa7 ♗xe4 22 ♖xe7 ♖fc8 23 ♘d4 ♖xc3 24 ♘b5 ♖c2 25 ♘d6 ♗d5 26 a4 ♖f8 27 h4 and White was better in Kalygin-Yagupov, Tula 2004) 17 ♕xb7 ♕xc4 18 ♖xd7 ♖fb8 19 ♕c7 ♕xc7 20 ♖xc7 ♘d5 21 ♖c5 a5 22 ♘d4 ♖c8 23 ♘c6 White had some winning chances in De Gleria-Kveinys, Essen 2001.

16...♗d7! *(D)*

This is based on the point that White can't now profitably capture the b7-pawn.

16...♖b8 is too passive. 17 ♖b4 ♕c6 18 ♕e3 b6 19 ♗d3 ♗b7 20 ♖g4 ♘f5 21 ♗xf5 exf5 22 ♘d4 ♕c8 23 ♖f4 g6 24 ♖h4 h5 25 ♖xh5 1-0, as in Nisipeanu-Ramirez Alvarez, Decameron 2003, is an unusually harsh punishment, but I think Black should avoid the whole line.

16...♕c6!? is a good alternative, dislodging the white queen from its strong post. 17 ♕d3 ♕c7 18 ♖fd1 b6 19 ♕d6 ♕xc4 20 ♕xe7 ♗a6 was fine for Black in Kristjansson-Lupulescu, Calvia Olympiad 2004.

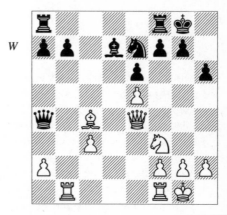

17 ♗d3

Mamedyarov just adores playing endgames, and has heavily structured his repertoire around them.

17 ♕xb7 ♕xc4 18 ♕xd7 ♘d5 is equal.

17...♕xe4 18 ♗xe4 ♗c6

This led to a draw in Adams-Tkachev, Cannes (rapid) 2001, and has been considered fine for Black since then. It's fascinating that, even in such a position, Mamedyarov manages to find a resource.

19 ♗xc6 bxc6 20 c4!

Simply taking the d5-square away from the black knight.

20 ♖b7 ♘d5 had equalized in the aforementioned rapid game, which concluded 21 c4 ♘c3 22 a3 ♖fb8 23 ♖c7 ♖c8 24 ♖b7 ♖cb8 25 ♖c7 ♖c8 26 ♖b7 ♖cb8 ½-½.

20...♖ab8

This is such a natural move it seems hard to criticize, but it could be a small error. Rogozenko suggests 20...♖fb8 as a better defensive chance.

21 ♖fd1 *(D)*

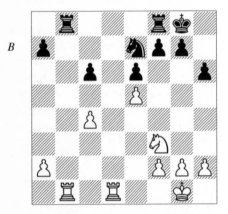

It may be hard to believe that Black can experience significant difficulties here, but Mamedyarov scores most of his points in less promising endgames than this. The seventh rank is weak and is about to be invaded by a white rook.

Mamedyarov is the foremost modern practitioner of what Botvinnik once called 'your own theory', namely the practice and study of positions which theory has rejected. Top chess trainer Mark Dvoretsky has written: "In general you need to be keen on your own pet lines, systems that you have analysed and have a feel for. A player who only knows what has been played before can scarcely count on success. He will never gain the advantage against an experienced opponent, since the latter will know it all too. But with the aid of 'your own theory', you can be a step ahead of your opponent in the

opening; you can put him in an uncomfortable position, take him into territory where he doesn't understand what is happening." Mamedyarov's games are a treasury of such instances and are well worth studying.

21...♖fd8 22 ♖xd8+ ♖xd8 23 h4!

Gaining kingside space, addressing back-rank concerns and preventing the typical plan of ...g5! and ...♘g6 to hit the e5-pawn.

23...♘f5 24 ♔f1 ♖d3 25 ♖b8+ ♔h7 26 ♖b7 ♘d4 27 ♘xd4 ♖d1+ 28 ♔e2 ♖xd4 *(D)*

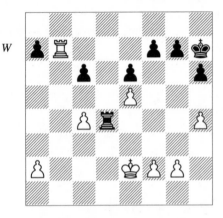

Rook and pawn endgames are notoriously complex. This one certainly favours White, though it seems that Berkes would not have lost with correct play.

29 ♖xf7 ♖xc4 30 ♖xa7 ♖xh4 31 ♔e3 ♖g4 32 ♖e7 ♔g6 33 ♔f3 ♖a4 34 g4 ♖xa2?

This seems to be the final mistake.

Rogozenko finds a draw for Black after 34...♖a3+! 35 ♔e4 (35 ♔g2 ♔g5 36 ♖xg7+ ♔f4 is at least equal for Black, since he's extremely active and the e5-pawn is dropping off) 35...♖a4+ 36 ♔f3 (36 ♔d3 ♖xg4 37 ♖xe6+ ♔f5) 36...♖a3+ 37 ♔f4 ♖xa2 38 f3 (38 ♖xe6+ ♔f7 and Black wins the f2-pawn – this is the point of enticing the white king to f4) 38...♖a4+ 39 ♔g3 ♖a5 40 f4 ♖a3+, when White should accept a draw by perpetual check, since ...♖f3 will follow ♔h4.

35 ♖xe6+ ♔g5 36 ♖xc6

The e-pawn is too strong.

36...♖a4 37 ♖c7 g6 38 ♖f7 ♖a3+ 39 ♔e4 ♔xg4 40 e6 ♖a1 41 ♔e5 h5 42 e7 ♖e1+ 43 ♔f6 h4 44 ♖f8 ♔f3 45 ♔g5+! 1-0

The h-pawn is worth a rook, but even this isn't enough to save the game. For instance, 45...♔g2 46 e8♕ ♖xe8 47 ♖xe8 h3 48 f4 h2 49 ♖h8 h1♕ 50 ♖xh1 ♔xh1 51 ♔xg6 is a trivial win.

Conclusions

1) This game details one of Black's best and most popular defensive systems. It can be reached via a number of move-orders.

2) White's best approach isn't clear. Mamedyarov's choice, heading straight for the endgame, worked well in this example, but the problem with such lines is that Black is half a step away from total equality. I'm not a fan of 9 ♕e2 and 10 ♕e4. Black is extremely solid, and White rarely threatens to take on d5 anyway. I recommend 9 ♖e1 followed by taking on d6 and playing the knight to c3. Black's most natural response lands him in a horrible position.

Game 3

Hrvoje Stević – Dimitrios Mastrovasilis
European Team Ch, Gothenburg 2005

1 e4 c5 2 c3 ♞f6 3 e5 ♞d5 4 d4 cxd4 5 ♞f3 e6 6 cxd4 d6 7 ♗c4 ♞b6 (D)

I disagree with Rogozenko that 7...♞c6 is superior – in my view, both continuations are of equal worth. For coverage of this alternative, see Game 2, Mamedyarov-Ramirez.

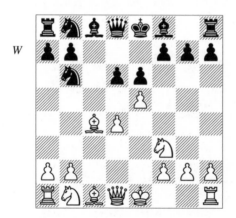

W

8 ♗b3

8 ♗d3 is also possible, but I'm not convinced by it since I think 8...♞c6 9 0-0 (9 a3 dxe5 10 dxe5 ♞d7! 11 ♗f4 ♞c5 is fine for Black, but 9 exd6 leads to pretty standard IQP fare) 9...♞b4! equalizes for Black.

8...dxe5

Played, in part, to entice the white knight to e5. Other moves:

a) 8...♞c6 9 exd6 ♕xd6 10 ♞c3 ♗e7 11 0-0 0-0 is a relatively favourable IQP position for

White since the black knight is poorly placed on b6.

b) 8...♗d7 9 0-0 ♗c6 was well dealt with in Pavasović-Ruck, European Team Ch, Plovdiv 2003: 10 ♞c3 ♗e7 11 exd6 ♕xd6 12 ♞e5 0-0 13 ♗f4 ♕d8 14 ♕g4! ♞8d7 15 ♗h6 ♗f6 16 ♞xc6 bxc6 17 ♗c2 ♖e8 18 ♞e4 g6 19 ♞d6 ♖e7 20 ♖fd1 with a clear advantage.

9 ♞xe5

Pretty much forced.

Naturally, 9 dxe5 doesn't give White anything – he can only demonstrate superiority in such positions with an initiative, and for this he needs much better development than he has here.

9...♞c6! (D)

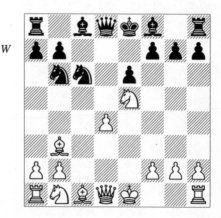

W

Black offers a structural change and simplification. It's natural to think that the forthcoming isolated pawn on c6 is a weakness, but this is only partly true. In fact, it's quite difficult to create genuine pressure on this pawn, while it gives Black three major pluses:

1) The prospect of play down the half-open b-file;

2) Total restraint of the d-pawn (the prospects of a killing d5 advance are virtually zero);

3) He has the option of playing ...c5 and eliminating the last white centre pawn.

That said, I think White retains a normal opening advantage – he has more space and his pieces will be more active for the foreseeable future. Black must be careful about making a ...c5 break, since White's pieces will generally be better placed to benefit from the opening of the position.

10 ♘xc6

While this splits Black's pawns, I think the main effect is to muzzle the d4-pawn.

10 ♘f3 is a more ambitious continuation. I tried this in Collins-Mogranzini, Turin Olympiad 2006, and while the game turned out badly, I had no complaints from the opening: 10...♗e7 11 ♘c3 ♗f6 12 ♗e3 ♘a5 13 ♗c2 ♘ac4 14 ♗c1 (Joel Benjamin suggested that White should just let Black take on e3, by 14 ♕e2 for instance, but I was happy with what I got in the game) 14...♘d6 15 0-0 0-0 16 ♕d3 g6 17 ♗h6 ♖e8 18 ♖ad1 ♘d5 19 ♗b3 ♘xc3 20 bxc3 b6 21 ♖fe1 ♗b7 22 ♘e5 ♖c8 23 ♕h3 ♗d5 24 ♖d3 b5 25 ♘g4 ♗xb3 and here I should have just recaptured on b3, with some initiative.

10...bxc6 11 0-0 ♗e7 *(D)*

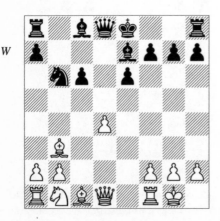

I'm reasonably sure this is the right square. Putting the bishop on d6 looks active, but there's no convincing follow-up and it's important to keep some pressure on the d-pawn so that the white queen is restricted.

12 ♘c3 0-0

Black basically has two ways to play this position. The first is to play for ...c5, eliminating both the black weakness on c6 and the white one on d4. The second, more ambitious, method is to keep the pawn-structure as it is. After all, the main threat from an isolated d-pawn (the d5-advance) is eliminated due to the c6-pawn.

13 ♕d3 *(D)*

This isn't the only option here, but is quite a logical one – White prepares to line up his queen and bishop with ♗c2, which will force ...g6 and allow the dark-squared bishop to shoot to h6.

13 ♗f4 a5 14 ♖e1 ♗a6 15 ♗c2 ♗c4 16 ♗e5 g6 17 ♖e3 ♘d7 18 ♗f4 ♘f6 19 b3 ♗d5 20 ♖h3 ♖e8 21 ♕d2 ♗f8 was played in Murariu-Antić, Budapest 2006. Then 22 ♗e5 leaves White slightly more active but Black remains very solid.

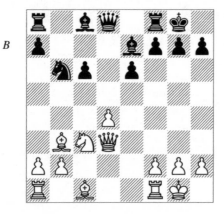

13...a5!

An excellent plan. The light-squared bishop can suffer in such a structure, because it is locked in by the c6- and e6-pawns. One method of resolving this is to play ...c5, but Mastrovasilis's move has two advantages:

1) It is easier to implement;

2) It activates the black rook down the a-file – now White will need to look out for ...a4 ideas.

The alternative plan of 13...c5 was tried in Okhotnik-Wittmann, Graz 2002, and proved to be a clean equalizer: 14 ♗c2 g6 15 dxc5 ♕xd3 16 ♗xd3 ♗xc5 17 ♗e4 ♗a6! 18 ♖d1 ♖ad8 with level play. This kind of stuff is typical after 10 ♘xc6, which is why I really don't like the move.

14 ♗c2 (D)

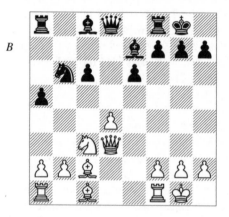

B

The bishop wasn't doing much on b3, so it retreats in order to force a kingside concession.

14...g6 15 ♖d1 ♗a6 16 ♕f3 ♖c8 17 ♗h6 ♖e8 18 ♖ac1

White's pieces are actively placed and he controls more space, so his position seems slightly preferable. In this particular structure, I think it makes sense to put the rooks on c1 and d1, since there is no chance of a breakthrough with d5 and Black has a weak pawn on c6.

Mastrovasilis now comes up with an inventive bishop manoeuvre:

18...♗c4! 19 b3 ♗d5

The problem bishop has found its way to an excellent square. The forthcoming exchange gives White the two bishops, but leaves Black with an unshakeable knight on d5.

20 ♘xd5

I don't really see the value in this – White can play it whenever he wants. Something like 20 ♕h3 would have kept some more tension in the position.

20...♘xd5 21 ♗d3 ♕b6 (D)

I'm not sure if Black is threatening to take on d4 right now, but it's certainly an idea which will feature in the forthcoming play.

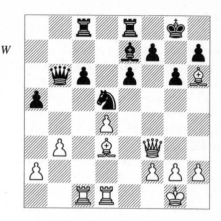

W

22 ♖c4 ♖ed8 23 g3 ♖d6

Another strong move, preparing ...♕d8, both defending the kingside and pressurizing the d-pawn.

24 h4

A natural idea to soften up the black kingside.

24...♕d8 25 h5 ♘b6 26 ♖cc1 ♘d5 27 ♖c4 ♗f6!?

Mastrovasilis is a promising young grandmaster who plays with a lot of composure and confidence. Here, he finds a good way to keep the game going, rather than consenting to a repetition with 27...♘b6.

28 ♗e4 ♗g7 29 ♗xg7 ♔xg7 30 h6+

As it turns out, this pawn drops off fairly quickly. However, White gets the a5-pawn in return, so nothing is spoiled yet.

30...♔f8 31 ♖c5 ♕g5 32 ♖xa5 ♕xh6 33 ♖a7 ♕g7 34 a4 ♘e7 35 a5 ♖xd4 36 a6 ♖cd8 (D)

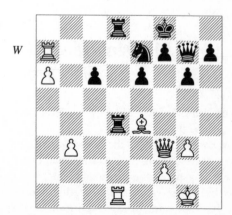

W

37 ♖e1?!

37 ♖xd4 ♕xd4 38 ♕e3!, as pointed out by Rogozenko, maintains the balance.

37...♕e5 38 ♖e3 ♖d1+ 39 ♔g2 ♕a1 40 ♔h2 ♕g7 41 ♕f4?

41 g4 keeps Black's advantage within manageable proportions.

41...g5! 42 ♕g4 f5 43 ♗xf5 exf5 44 ♕h3 ♖1d7 45 ♖xd7 ♖xd7

The extra piece is completely decisive. The length of the game can be explained, in part, by the match circumstances – this was a team championship, and it's incumbent upon all team members to stay on the board for as long as possible so that team-mates don't get discouraged.

46 ♖e6 ♖d2 47 ♕f1 ♕d4 48 ♖e2 ♖xe2 49 ♕xe2 ♔e8 50 ♔g2 (D)

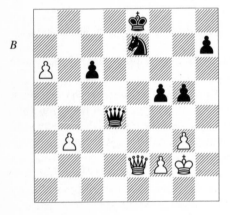

50...♔d7

White's only (slight) chance in this position is his a-pawn – it's never going to queen, but it could prove a sufficient distraction to prevent the black pieces from adequately defending their king or their kingside. With this in mind, Mastrovasilis moves his king across to cover.

51 ♕a2 ♘c8 52 ♕a3 g4 53 ♕f8 ♔c7 54 ♔g1

54 ♕xf5? ♕d5+ 55 ♕xd5 cxd5 is a trivial win.

54...♕a1+ 55 ♔h2 ♕xa6 56 ♕xf5 ♕e2 57 ♕xh7+ ♔b6 58 ♕f5 ♘d6 59 ♕f8 ♔c5 60 b4+ ♔d5 61 ♕g8+ ♔d4 62 ♕g7+ ♔c4 63 ♕f6 ♕d2 64 ♕e6+ ♔b5 65 ♕xg4 ♕xf2+ 66 ♔h1 ♕f1+ 67 ♔h2 ♕f2+ 68 ♔h1 ♘f5 69 ♕g5 ♕f1+ 70 ♔h2 ♕f2+ 71 ♔h1 c5! 0-1

An elegant finish.

Conclusions

1) 7...♘b6 is one of Black's more attractive defences in the c3 Sicilian. He gets a solid position with chances to play for the full point.

2) On move 10 White has an important choice to make. It seems counterintuitive to retreat the knight rather than compromise Black's pawns, but 10 ♘f3 certainly gives White the attacking chances typical of an IQP – his loss of time is compensated by the poor black knight on b6.

3) 10 ♘xc6 leads to a positional game where Black has a choice of ways to handle the position. The less ambitious is to play for ...c5 and try to equalize. If you want to play for a win, the alternative plan with ...a5 is well worth considering, since a lot of tension remains in the position and White needs some skill to place his pieces correctly.

Game 4

Miroslav Marković – Sergei Rublevsky

Serbian Team Ch, Budva 2004

1 e4 c5 2 c3 ♘f6 3 e5 ♘d5 4 ♘f3 e6 5 d4 cxd4 6 cxd4 d6 (D)

Rublevsky also plays the white side of this system. It has grown in popularity, mainly because it is viewed as a legitimate winning attempt for Black – mass simplification will be unlikely. That said, mass simplification is a pretty good way of ensuring that you don't lose the game, so this plan comes with a certain level of risk.

7 a3

Preparing the development of the bishop to d3 in the short term, and play on the queenside in the longer term.

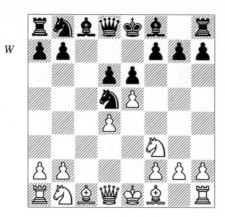

After 7 ♗d3, 7...公b4! is a clean equalizer. However, it is still important to be vigilant, as is painfully illustrated by McShane-Collins, Kilkenny 2002: 8 ♗b5+!? (I think this is the best attempt to disrupt Black's coordination, though it shouldn't be enough to disturb the theoretical verdict of equality) 8...♗d7 9 ♗c4 ♗c6 10 0-0 公d7 11 公c3!? (11 exd6 ♗xd6 is fine for Black) 11...♗xf3!? (this isn't forced, but is by no means bad if followed up correctly) 12 ♕xf3 公c2? (I think 12...公c6 is fine for Black; the fact that after the text-move I even considered 13 ♖b1?? 公xd4 is indicative of a rather desperate mindset; Luke had other ideas) 13 d5!! (this central breakthrough may not win on the spot, but I think that White has a clear advantage in all variations and this, combined with the practical shock of facing such a move over the board, renders Black's defensive task hopeless) 13...公d4 (desperately trying to regain control of some central squares; 13...公xa1 14 dxe6 fxe6 15 ♗xe6 公xe5 16 ♕e2 ♗e7 17 ♗e3 ♔f8 18 ♖xa1 gives White magnificent compensation for the exchange) 14 ♕g4 dxe5 15 dxe6 fxe6 16 ♗e3 公f6 17 ♕h3 ♕b6 18 ♗xd4! (blasting through the centre in straightforward fashion) 18...exd4 19 ♖fe1 ♗e7 20 ♖xe6 ♕c5 21 ♖ae1 dxc3 22 ♖xe7+ ♕xe7 23 ♖xe7+ ♔xe7 24 ♕e6+ ♔d8 25 ♕d6+ ♔e8 26 ♗b5+ ♔f7 27 ♕c7+ 1-0.

7...♗d7!

Starting a compact development – the bishop is going to c6, and the knight to d7. It makes sense to delay the development of the f8-bishop so that White is discouraged from exd6.

8 ♗d3 ♗c6 9 0-0 公d7 (D)

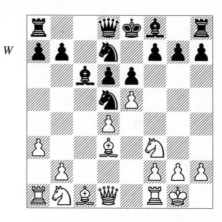

The black position doesn't present any easy targets. With a pawn on e5, White would normally be tempted to start a kingside attack, but Black hasn't castled yet (and, due to the clustering in the centre, he won't be forced to castle any time soon) so such play would be futile. Play in the centre is also problematic, since Black has so much control over the d5- and e5-squares. This leaves the queenside as a natural forum for White's ambitions.

10 b4

White seizes some space on the queenside and threatens to trap the bishop. Yudin-Kornev, Moscow (Aeroflot Open) 2006 featured more mundane play: 10 ♗d2 dxe5 11 dxe5 ♗e7 12 公c3 公xc3 13 ♗xc3 公c5 14 ♗c2 ♕xd1 15 ♖fxd1 and White had nothing in the endgame.

10...a6

Dealing with the threat, but there's an ulterior motive...

11 ♕e2

Black would otherwise have seriously considered ...♗b5!? at some point – the light-squared bishops come off, and ♗xb5 axb5 is an unclear structural transformation, since Black's pawns are weakened but he gets a half-open a-file and the c4-square for his knight.

That said, in Tiviakov-Bosch, Dutch Ch, Hilversum 2006, after 11 公bd2 Black didn't take my brilliant positional advice. After 11...dxe5 12 dxe5 公c3?! 13 ♕c2 ♖c8 14 ♕xc3 ♗xf3 15 ♕d4 ♗d5 16 公e4 ♗e7 17 ♖e1 0-0 18 ♗f4 a5 19 公d6 ♗xd6 20 exd6 axb4 21 axb4 ♕b6 22

Wxb6 ♘xb6 23 ♖ac1 White had a clear advantage in the endgame due to his bishop-pair and d6-pawn.

11...♗e7 12 ♖e1 ♖c8 13 ♖a2!? *(D)*

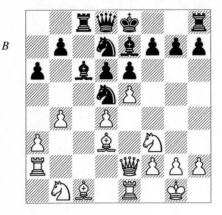

This is a typical development – it's hard to take care of the b1-knight and c1-bishop, so the rook swings across to grab some squares.

13...♘7b6 14 ♖c2 0-0

Finally getting his rook into play at the cost of giving White a target.

15 h4!?

With so many black pieces on the queenside, and the e5-pawn acting as a wedge, White's chances clearly lie on the kingside and this move is designed to increase those prospects, first by gaining control of the g5-square and second by introducing the idea of h5-h6.

15...dxe5 16 dxe5 Wd7 17 ♗g5 ♖fd8 18 ♖d2 h6 19 ♗e3 ♘a4

The position is now a tough positional struggle of which a formal assessment is elusive.

20 ♘d4!?

This is an enterprising pawn sacrifice. Rublevsky likes taking pawns, so...

20...♘xe3 21 Wxe3 ♗xh4 22 ♗c2 ♘b6 23 ♘f5 *(D)*

This always signals a strong attack, but it seems that Black can defend.

23...♘d5 24 ♘xh6+!? ♔f8!

24...gxh6 25 Wxh6 is excellent for White – of course, the bishop can't be saved due to mate.

25 Wh3 ♗g5 26 ♘g4

26 ♘f5 exf5 27 ♗xf5 Wc7 is bad for White.

26...♔e7

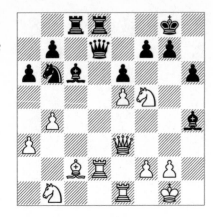

Rublevsky declines the exchange. 26...♗xd2 27 ♘xd2 leads to fascinating complications, with one illustrative line being 27...♘e7 28 ♘c4 Wd4 29 Wh8+ ♘g8 30 ♘ce3 ♗e4 31 ♖d1 ♗xc2! 32 ♖xd4 ♖xd4 33 ♘f6!? gxf6 34 exf6 ♗g6 and White seems to be in trouble.

27 ♘e3 Wc7

27...♖h8 28 Wg3 just helps White.

28 Wg3 ♗h6

28...♗xe3? would be a dubious positional decision, since after 29 fxe3 there are four factors in White's favour:

1) The g7-pawn is in need of protection;

2) The d5-knight can be kicked with e4;

3) The half-open f-file can be used by the rooks;

4) The h-file has no obstructions, so the white queen may be able to penetrate down this line.

29 Wh4+ ♔e8

Even with hindsight, it's hard to say whether this is better than 29...♔f8.

30 ♘c4 *(D)*

30 ♘xd5 ♗xd5 31 f4 is the alternative, but White can be forgiven for getting squeamish about the a7-g1 diagonal.

30...♗b5

30...We7 is a good defence, bringing the queen to the aid of the king.

31 ♘d6+ ♖xd6 32 exd6 Wxd6

Black immediately regains the exchange.

33 ♗b3

33 ♗d3 ♗xd2 34 ♗xb5+ axb5 35 ♘xd2 is another attempt, but after 35...Wf4! White lacks full compensation.

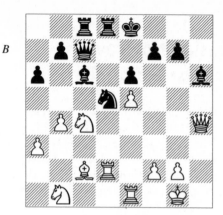

33...♗xd2 34 ♘xd2 ♘f6 35 ♘f3?

White would have been better served by the creative 35 ♕h8+! ♕f8 36 ♕h2!, when the passivity of Black's pieces, together with the slight weakness of his king, is worth a pawn.

35...♗d7 36 ♘d4 ♔f8 37 ♖d1 ♕e5 38 ♘f3 ♕c3 39 ♘d4 *(D)*

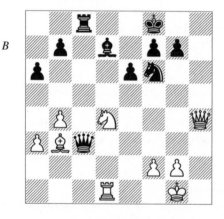

This is a very difficult position to judge. White has compensation for the pawn, though it seems to be insufficient.

39...♔g8 40 ♕f4 ♕c7 41 ♕g5 ♖d8 42 ♖d3 ♖c8 43 ♗c2 ♘e4?

43...e5 is better: 44 ♘f5 (44 ♖g3 ♘e8 45 ♘f5 ♕xc2 46 ♘e7+ ♔f8 47 ♘xc8 f6 48 ♕h5 ♗xc8 is winning for Black) 44...♗xf5 45 ♕xf5 e4 and Black is dominating.

44 ♕h4 f5??

It was better just to drop the exposed knight back.

45 ♘xf5!

Finally!

45...♕xc2

45...exf5 46 ♗b3+ is decisive.

46 ♘e7+ ♔f7 *(D)*

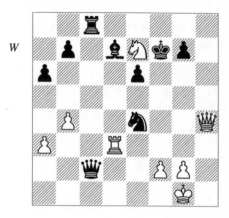

47 ♖xd7

Material is equal, but Black is about to start shedding some.

47...♕c1+ 48 ♔h2 ♖h8 49 ♘f5+ ♔g6 50 ♕xh8 1-0

This is a typical battle in the ...e6 and ...d6 system – immense complications, mutual mistakes and winning prospects for both sides. Even with computerized assistance, it's hard to find the objective truth about such positions.

Conclusions

1) The ...e6 and ...d6 defence is quite an ambitious one. Black doesn't attempt to simplify the position, which is the safest way to play a position where one has a substantial space disadvantage. I like to think of this line as similar to the Sicilian Scheveningen – Black needs to be prepared to face an attack, but if he's able to repel it then he will have his chance to win the game.

2) The 7 a3 system, one of White's two main attempts, is quite a positional line which can be handled in a variety of ways. Seizing space on the queenside with b4 is a natural idea, but White could also aim for simple play in the centre. Black's piece formation in response, with the bishop on c6 and knights on d5 and d7, is extremely solid.

Game 5

Ildar Khairullin – Stanislav Novikov

Russian Junior Ch, Noiabrsk 2005

1 e4 c5 2 c3 ᐸf6 3 e5 ᐸd5 4 d4 cxd4 5 ᐸf3 e6 6 cxd4 b6 *(D)*

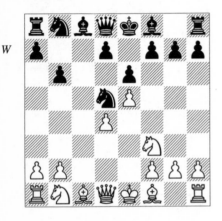

This was Gallagher's main recommendation in his anti-Sicilians book. Black prepares to develop his queen's bishop, either to b7 or a6. This is a laudable aim, but there's no early pressure on the white centre. Before we examine the specifics, here is a brief summary:

1) Black needs to play very accurately in this line;

2) Black is under pressure in several key variations.

So I wouldn't advise Black to go in for this continuation.

7 ᐸc3

Offering an exchange which will have important implications for the middlegame.

7 ᙵd3 is a simple developing move and, in my opinion, is more promising than the text-move. After 7...ᙵa6 8 0-0 ᙵe7 9 ᐸc3 ᐸxc3 10 bxc3 ᙵxd3 11 ᙿxd3 we examine:

a) 11...d5?! is a mistake which has been made by quite a few decent players. After 12 exd6 ᙿxd6?, White has 13 ᙵa3! since Black must watch out for ᙿe4 winning the rook on a8. Following 13...ᙿc7 14 ᙵxe7 ᙶxe7 15 ᙲfe1, White will make the d5 advance, with an overwhelming game.

b) On 11...0-0, White has 12 d5 exd5 13 ᙿxd5 (or 13 ᙲd1 ᐸc6 14 ᙿxd5) 13...ᐸc6 (13...ᐸa6 might be better, aiming for the c5-square) 14 ᙲd1 ᙿc7 15 ᙵf4 ᙲfd8 16 ᙿe4 with strong pressure. I really think Black should avoid this position, but it has been quite extensively tested.

7...ᐸxc3

Such exchanges can have two implications, and it's worth considering both:

Piece Reduction: Black has less space, so an exchange of knights will generally be in his favour. In addition, the white knight is a potentially dangerous piece, especially if it gets to g5 via e4. However, the knight on d5 controlled some useful dark squares and was a good piece in its own right. In conclusion, the piece reduction analysis shows that, on balance, Black should exchange on c3.

Structure: What are the ramifications of bringing the white b-pawn to c3?

1) Black is given a target down the half-open c-file.

2) The white centre is strengthened in two respects: the d-pawn is now more secure than before; and White now has the option of playing c4, which controls d5 and gives him the option of further play in the centre.

In my opinion, taking on c3 is an ambitious way to play the position from a structural perspective, since White is given a potential weakness but can also generate interesting and threatening play.

7...ᙵb7 is also possible; the position after 8 ᙵd3 is frequently reached by a 7 ᙵd3 move-order. After 8...ᙵe7 9 0-0 0-0, White can retain the knights with 10 ᐸe4, while 10 ᙿe2 ᐸxc3 11 bxc3 d6 12 exd6 ᙿxd6 leads to a tricky position. White's main idea is to play ᐸg5, forcing the weakening of the black kingside or else securing the two bishops. However, Rozentalis and Harley show that 13 ᐸg5 h6 14 ᐸh7?! (dropping back to e4 is much sounder) 14...ᙲc8 leaves White in trouble, since the most aggressive continuation of 15 ♕g4 ♔h8 16 ♕h5? ♖xc3 17 ♗xh6 ♕d5 wins for Black.

8 bxc3 ♕c7! *(D)*

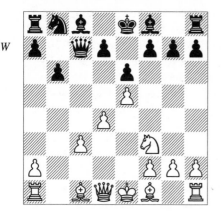

W

Trying to gain some time on the c3-pawn, though White isn't forced to defend it.

9 ♗d2

Not the best square for the bishop by any means, but at least the pawns remain equal.

9 ♗e2!? is a more dynamic way to handle the position. After 9...♕xc3+ 10 ♗d2 ♕c7 (10...♕a3 has been tried with more success) 11 ♖c1 ♘c6 12 0-0 ♗b7 13 d5! exd5 14 ♗f4 White had interesting compensation in Sermek-Medvegy, Cairo 2001.

9...d6 10 ♗d3 ♘d7

It's pretty clear that this (with ...♘d7 and ...♗b7) is the tightest defensive set-up for Black.

11 ♘g5!?

This is extremely aggressive, and invites huge complications. 11 0-0 ♗b7 gives White some alternative options but none seem to promise much; for instance, 12 ♖e1 dxe5 13 ♘xe5 ♘xe5 14 ♖xe5 ♗d6 15 ♖h5 g6 16 ♖h3 and now Black's best is the cool-headed 16...0-0! with no problems.

11...♗b7 12 0-0 *(D)*

This position is often reached via the move-order 10...♗b7 11 0-0 ♘d7 12 ♘g5.

12...dxe5 13 ♕h5 g6 14 ♕h3 ♗e7

White now has a major choice.

15 ♖fe1

15 ♖ae1!? is an extremely dangerous continuation, and indicative of the kind of tough

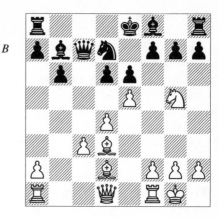

B

defensive task which this line entails for Black. 15...♗d5 16 f4! exd4 17 cxd4 ♗c4 18 f5! gives a very strong attack.

15...♗d5 16 ♖ac1

16 f4!? has also been tested, but without any clear verdict. I wouldn't be wild about defending the black side without thorough preparation.

16...♗c4

This is actually a pretty good move, though I can understand if anyone doesn't like the look of the position Black gets in a couple of moves.

17 ♕f3

This forks the a8-rook and the f7-pawn.

17...0-0 *(D)*

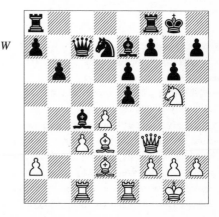

W

The only move.

18 ♘xf7!

Taking advantage of the unprotected rook on a8.

18...♗xd3

I think this is slightly inaccurate. 18...♖ac8 19 ♘h6+ ♔h8 20 ♕h3 ♗xd3 21 ♕xd3 gains a useful tempo compared to the game.

19 ♘h6+ ♔h8 20 ♕xd3

White must have some advantage here.

20...♗f6!? 21 ♘g4 ♗g7

Black has 'fianchettoed by hand', which has shored up his king position a little.

22 ♕g3

22 ♗h6 looks standard, exchanging off the fianchettoed bishop and weakening the black king. Maybe White avoided it due to 22...♗xh6 23 ♘xh6 ♖f4!?, intending ...♖af8 with play on the f-file, but after 24 ♘g4! ♖af8 25 f3 I like White.

22...♕c4! 23 ♘xe5 ♘xe5 24 dxe5 ♕xa2 25 ♗e3 ♕c4 (D)

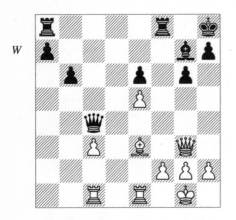

This position seems balanced. Black still has some concerns over his king safety, but the passed a-pawn is a major asset.

26 ♗d4 ♕c6 27 ♕e3 ♖fb8 28 ♖b1 ♖b7 29 h4

Starting some useful play on the kingside. Of course, the chances of a mating attack are extremely slim, but by reducing the pawn-cover around the black king, White increases the chances of perpetual check (especially if Black uses all his pieces to try to force through his queenside majority).

29...b5 30 ♕h3 a5 31 h5 gxh5 32 ♕xh5 a4 33 ♕e2 a3 34 ♕a2 ♗f8 35 f4 ♖f7 36 ♖f1 ♕c4 37 ♕xc4 bxc4

The position has turned and is now better for Black, but White defends stubbornly.

38 ♖f2 h5 39 g3 ♔h7 40 ♔g2 ♗h6 41 ♗e3 ♖d7 42 ♗d4 ♖f7 43 ♗e3 ♖d8 44 ♗d4 h4 45 gxh4 ♖xf4 46 ♖xf4 ♗xf4 47 ♖a1 ♖a8 48 ♔f3 ♗h6 49 ♗c5 ♖a5 50 ♗b4 ♖xe5 51 ♖xa3 ♔g6 52 ♖a5 ♖xa5 53 ♗xa5

White still must play with some care, since the e-pawn is much stronger than the h-pawn and he has a weakness on c3.

53...♔f5 54 ♗b4 e5 55 ♗a5 ♗g7

After 55...e4+ 56 ♔e2 ♔g4 57 ♗d8 White seems to hold.

56 ♗b4 ♗f6 57 h5 ♗g7 58 ♔e2 ♗h6 59 ♗d6 e4 60 ♗c5 ♔g4 61 ♗e3 ♗g7 62 ♗d2 ♔xh5 ½-½

63 ♔e3 ♗h6+ 64 ♔xe4 ♗xd2 65 ♔d4 is as drawn as it gets. A hard-fought game.

Conclusions

1) I don't like this line for Black. I used to play it myself and found White's attacking chances just too much. It's as if White has a great IQP position, with masses of activity but without as much structural weakness. Of course, this is a personal opinion, and the system is undoubtedly playable, but I'm putting a health warning on it.

2) I recommend 7 ♗d3 over 7 ♘c3. There is no need to give Black a structural target right away, and the position after move 12 in the 7 ♗d3 line is extremely pleasant for White.

3) In the line with 7 ♘c3 ♘xc3, it's important for Black to remember to flick in 8...♕c7 to gain some time. I'm not convinced by White's attempt to sacrifice a pawn on move 9, so he should probably settle for 9 ♗d2.

4) On move 11 in the main line, I recommend the extremely aggressive 11 ♘g5!?. The alternatives don't seem to give much, while freeing the f-pawn and the queen leads to a lot of promising attacking options.

2 2...♘f6: Main Line with 6 ♗c4

1 e4 c5 2 c3 ♘f6 3 e5 ♘d5 4 d4 cxd4 5 ♘f3

5 ♕xd4 is a radical way of avoiding the cxd4 structure. White's queen is aggressively placed, but his second move is looking rather pointless. Game 9, Deviatkin-Macieja, is a recent and mutually creative game in this line between two good GMs.

5...♘c6 6 ♗c4

Immediately putting the bishop on a dangerous diagonal. Black needs to play accurately in order to neutralize this piece.

6...♘b6

Black can also play 6...e6, when 7 cxd4 d6 transposes to Game 2, Mamedyarov-Ramirez.

7 ♗b3

Now Black can take on c3, but that's extremely risky since the game opens up to White's benefit. Instead, he normally picks one of two alternative plans.

7...g6

This is the most ambitious idea, preparing a kingside fianchetto.

7...d5 is a more reliable equalizing attempt, looking to develop the light-squared bishop and exchange pieces. It has been extensively explored and can be considered a 'safe line'. Game 6, Erenburg-Mikhalevski, is one of the more interesting recent tussles in this line.

After 7...g6:

8 ♘g5 is extremely sharp, immediately attacking the f7-pawn. Game 7, Zhigalko-Khairullin, is an interesting game here between two young talented players.

8 cxd4 is a quieter option which promises good chances of an edge. Game 8, Baklan-Romero, is a model demonstration of White's chances here.

Game 6
Sergei Erenburg – Viktor Mikhalevski
Beersheba 2003

1 e4 c5 2 c3 ♘f6 3 e5 ♘d5 4 d4 cxd4 5 ♘f3 ♘c6 6 ♗c4 ♘b6 7 ♗b3 *(D)*

This has built up a substantial body of theory, but has never really been shown to lead to anything for White. All of the leading experts in the c3 Sicilian are now focusing their attention elsewhere. Nonetheless, it's an important line to get to grips with.

7...d5

This is the most reliable defence. Black compels the exchange of the e5-pawn and brings his queen's bishop into the game, so that it can neutralize its white counterpart by ...♗e6.

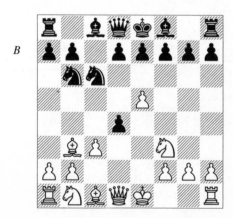

Simple kingside development with, say, 7...e6 and 8...♗e7, does nothing to contest White's space advantage, and leaves Black with absolutely no prospects.

I should mention that 7...d6 gives White the option of transposing into the 5 cxd4 d6 6 ♗c4 ♘b6 7 ♗b3!? line, though if White wanted to play this he probably would have adopted the mainstream move-order.

7...dxc3 doesn't necessarily lose on the spot, but it's extremely risky. Black is a long way from completing development and White can use the interim period to generate a substantial initiative. Nunn gives 8 ♘xc3 g6 (8...e6 9 ♘e4 leaves White in full control of the d6-square, which makes the development of the c8-bishop extremely awkward, given that it can't be fianchettoed since the b6-knight stands in the way) 9 0-0 ♗g7 10 ♕e2 0-0 11 ♖d1, concluding that "White has strong pressure. Black can hardly free himself without returning the pawn, but then White's active pieces tend to give him the advantage."

The enterprising 7...g6!? is covered in the next game.

8 exd6

If White doesn't take, Black will play ...♗g4 and ...e6, with an excellent version of the French since his bishop is outside the pawn-chain.

8...♕xd6 *(D)*

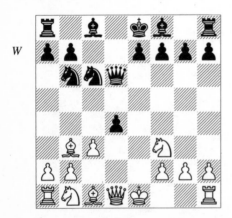

The standard advice against bringing out one's queen at an early stage is useful one to bear in mind – certainly, in these lines, Black's queen can become a target for the white pieces.

Nonetheless, he has a good developmental idea – ...♗e6!, which will exchange the strong b3-bishop and allow the a8-rook into play. It's quite rare that someone should complete his queenside development while still being three moves away from castling, but practice has established this approach as the most accurate.

9 0-0

Bringing the rook into the game and ensuring that the king is not harassed.

9 ♘a3 was one of the main attempts to cause problems for Black here, once it became apparent that the main line is just a draw. Black's best approach is to exploit the fact that ♘xc3 is unavailable by playing 9...dxc3!. White now has a choice – queens on or queens off:

a) 10 ♕e2 ♗f5 11 ♘b5 ♕d7 12 ♘e5 ♘xe5 13 ♕xe5 and now 13...♖c8 was an invention of English GM Peter Wells. White is now struggling to demonstrate enough for the pawn. Capturing on a7 is dubious since Black gains excellent play by taking on b2 and playing ...♘c4.

b) After 10 ♕xd6 exd6 11 ♘b5 we have an extremely difficult queenless middlegame, in which both sides have threats. Rogozenko recommends 11...♖b8 12 bxc3 (12 ♘g5 ♘e5 is fine for Black) 12...♗e7 13 ♗f4 0-0 with equality.

9...♗e6 *(D)*

Exchanging off a key white piece. Alternative approaches don't inspire confidence – for instance, the simple 9...e6 leaves Black very passively placed.

9...dxc3 is also a dubious option – White has a substantial endgame initiative after both 10 ♕xd6 exd6 11 ♘xc3 and 10 ♘xc3 ♕xd1 11 ♖xd1. In the former case, the poor black structure is a major factor, while in the latter, White has moves such as ♘d5 and ♗e3 at his disposal.

10 ♗xe6

This is White's last major opportunity to deviate from the drawish main line.

Here also 10 ♘a3 has been tried. After 10...dxc3! 11 ♕e2 ♗xb3 12 ♘b5 ♕b8 13 axb3 Black has tried to develop his bishop by two methods: 13...e5 (13...g6!? is more ambitious) 14 bxc3 ♗e7 and now Smagin's 15 ♗g5 could be the most promising. After 15...a6 16 ♗xe7

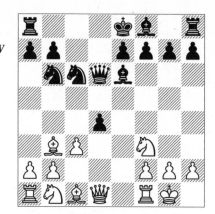

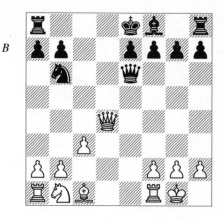

⛁xe7 17 ⛁xe5! the knight on b5 is untouchable, and following 17...0-0 (Rogozenko thinks the materialistic 17...f6 is not worth the risk since the black king is exposed to a vicious attack) 18 ⛁d4 White might have a slight edge.

10...♛xe6

Black definitely needs some skill or some theoretical knowledge to handle this position, since the development of his f8-bishop is far from straightforward.

11 ⛁xd4

11 cxd4 is a strategically dubious decision in my view – without a light-squared bishop White has fewer chances of generating an attack in the resulting IQP position, while Black is closer to a favourable late middlegame/endgame.

11...⛁xd4

This is the main move, but activates the white pieces so Black must know what he's doing. 11...♛d7 is a good alternative, which has an additional benefit of being less explored than 11...⛁xd4.

12 ♛xd4 *(D)*

Black's only concern is his development. The pawn-structure is more than OK for him, since his extra central pawn will be extremely useful in any middlegame and most endgames.

12...♜d8 13 ♛h4!

This looks like the only good square for the queen.

13...♛c6!?

An interesting idea from Mikhalevski, keeping the queen on a safe and strong square while preparing to get his dark-squared bishop out and castle.

13...♛e2 has been the main line for a long time, and looks completely adequate. The line has some emotional significance for me since a win with the black pieces here enabled me to become Irish Champion in 2002. 14 ⛁d2 and now:

a) 14...♜xd2 15 ⛃xd2 ♛xd2 16 ♜fd1 ♛h6 17 ♛g3 ♛c6 is simply a draw in all lines – as an example, have a look at 18 ♛b8+ ⛁c8 19 b4 e6 20 a4 ⛃e7 21 b5 ♛c5 22 ♛xb7 0-0 23 a5 ⛃f6 24 b6 axb6 25 a6 ⛃xc3 26 a7 ⛁xa7 with equality, Malaniuk-Azmaiparashvili, Tallinn 1981.

b) 14...h5!? is a really nice positional move, trying to exchange queens and bring the h8-rook into play after ...♛g4. 15 a4 (a good move – White had previously played 15 h3 but I think this idea is very logical, since White activates his rook down the a-file) 15...♛g4 16 ♛xg4 hxg4 *(D)*.

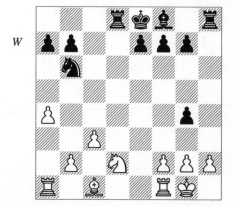

I was very happy with this structural change, since the knight is denied the f3-square and the h2-pawn can easily come under attack. 17 a5 ♘d5 18 ♖a4! (a creative way to bring the rook into play) 18...f5!? (dropping the knight back to f6 is simpler and, perhaps, sounder, but this move is far more ambitious; I got the formation I wanted in the game, though I wasn't so keen on dropping a pawn to achieve it!) 19 ♖e1 g6 20 ♘b3 ♔f7 21 c4 ♘f6 22 ♗e3 e5! (it's not worth trying to hold the queenside) 23 ♗xa7 ♘e4 24 ♖aa1 ♗b4 (all the black pieces are perfectly placed, and I think he has full compensation) 25 ♖ed1 f4 (maybe this is asking too much of the position; 25...♔e6 is a good alternative) 26 ♗b6 ♖xd1+ 27 ♖xd1 ♔e6 28 f3 gxf3 29 gxf3 ♘g5 30 ♔g2?! (30 ♖d3 is sounder, when 30...♖c8 31 c5 ♖h8!? 32 ♔g2 ♔f5 33 ♘c1 doesn't give Black enough compensation) 30...♘xf3 31 ♗c5?? (31 ♔xf3 ♖h3+ 32 ♔e4 ♖xb3 33 ♖d5 still leaves Black struggling) 31...♖xh2+ 32 ♔xf3 ♔f5! (a really satisfying move to play, even if it could be played by a 5-year-old; the threat of mate costs White material) 33 ♘d4+? (33 ♖d5 ♖h3+ 34 ♔f2 ♖xb3 is clearly better for Black, but White had to try this) 33...exd4 34 ♖xd4 ♖f2+! 0-1 Brady-Collins, Irish Ch, Greystones 2002. White loses both his pieces.

14 ♖e1 *(D)*

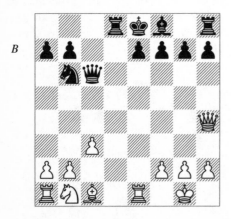

Black's basic problem, of course, is the development of his bishop. Once this piece gets into the game, White will have absolutely no advantage – moreover, because Black has an extra central pawn, the middlegame should be more pleasant for him. Extra central pawns

can be used ambitiously (...e5-e4-e3, winning squares and space) or defensively (a pawn on e6 cuts out any attacks along the a2-g8 diagonal). Mikhalevski decides to be bold:

14...f6!?

Mikhalevski's comment on this ambitious move is instructive: "Playing Sergei for the first time several years ago I was thinking about this move in a similar position during the game. That time I decided to play the standard 14...e6. This time I decided to surprise my young opponent. The idea of this move is pretty simple. I want to play ...e5 and then to finish development by means of ...♗e7 and ...0-0. At the same time I have been preventing ♗g5, which is possible after 14...e6."

I've annotated this move as interesting because I have great admiration for any professional player who, despite being aware of a safe equalizing line, decides on a more ambitious continuation. That said, from an objective standpoint Black seems to be asking too much of the position – in numerous lines, after logical play, his position simply splits down the middle.

14...e6 15 ♗g5 ♖d5 (not 15...f6?? 16 ♗xf6!) is the alternative – theory states that Black has a perfectly acceptable position.

15 ♘d2 e5 16 ♘f3 *(D)*

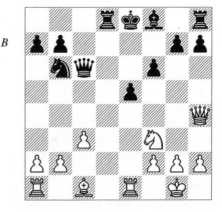

16...♗e7

Mikhalevski suggests 16...♗c5!? 17 ♕h5+ g6 18 ♕h6 ♖d7 as a good alternative. That may be the case, but it seems like Black is risking a lot for very little potential reward. After something

like 19 ♗f4 ♗d6 20 ♗g3 ♔f7!? his position is
playable, but I prefer White.

17 ♕h5+

Forcing an additional kingside weakness.

17...g6 18 ♕h3

The queen is superbly placed here, hitting h7
while eyeing the weak light squares on the h3-
c8 diagonal.

18...0-0?

Mikhalevski completely missed White's next
move.

He suggests 18...h5, intending to exchange
queens with 19...♕c8, because the immediate
18...♕c8 allows 19 ♕h6. Black's position creates a very dubious impression, but I don't see a
knockout punch for White. After 19 ♕g3 g5 20
♗xg5!? ♖g8, Mikhalevski gives 21 ♘xe5 and
assesses the position as unclear, but he doesn't
mention 21 ♕h3! fxg5 22 ♖xe5 g4 23 ♕h4!!
with an extremely strong attack.

19 ♘d4!

Without this resource, White could only beg
for a draw.

19...exd4?!

This might be a fatal error.

Erenburg's suggestion of 19...♕c4 walks a
tightrope. The idea is to meet ♘e6 with ...♖d3.
After 20 b3 ♕a6 21 ♘e6 ♖d3 22 ♗e3 ♖f7 23
♘c7 and Black is over the abyss, but White
doesn't appear to have a clear win.

20 ♖xe7

Forcing an unpleasant kingside weakening.

20...h5 21 ♕g3!?

Forcing a further weakening of the kingside.
Mikhalevski suggests the simple 21 ♕d3 f5 22
cxd4 winning a pawn.

21...f5

21...g5?? 22 ♗xg5! is trivial.

22 ♕e5 ♖f7

22...♕f6 is more compliant: 23 ♕xf6 ♖xf6
24 ♗g5 ♖fd6 25 ♖xb7 dxc3!? (25...♖8d7 26
♖xd7 ♖xd7 27 cxd4 ♖xd4 is a lost endgame) 26
♗xd8 cxb2 27 ♖b1 ♖xd8 28 g3 doesn't give
Black enough for the exchange.

23 ♖e6 (D)

It looks like Black can resign, but he imagi-
natively uses the one downside to White's position – the back rank.

23...dxc3!

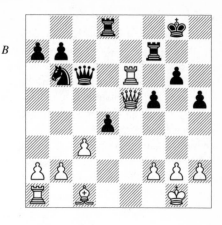

Mate threat number one.

24 ♗g5 c2

Mate threat number two! Erenburg must have
been totally confused by this point, and he immediately made an error.

25 ♖f1?

This is an extremely natural move, but it
throws away the win, which is to be had by 25
♖e1! ♘c4 26 ♕e2! (this is given as winning by
Fritz; Mikhalevski points out 26 ♕c3 ♕xe6 27
♖xe6 {it's better to take the rook on d8, but
White has no advantage in any case} 27...♖d1+
28 ♖e1 f4! and the c-pawn queens) 26...♖d6 27
♖e8+ ♔h7 28 b3 and the knight can't move in
view of the crushing ♕e5.

25...♘c4 26 ♖xc6

26 ♕e2 is no better: 26...♖d6 27 ♖xd6 ♘xd6
28 ♖c1 ♖c7 29 ♗f4 forces the return of the c2-
pawn, but nothing more: 29...♖c8 30 ♗xd6
♕xd6 31 ♖xc2 ♖xc2 32 ♕xc2 is a draw.

26...♘xe5 27 ♖xc2

Now we have a little jockeying for position,
but neither side has any real chance of generating anything.

**27...♖d5 28 ♗d2 ♘c6 29 ♖e1 ♖fd7 30 ♗c3
♔f7 31 ♔f1 ♘d4 32 ♖d2 ♘b5 33 ♖xd5 ♖xd5
34 ♗b4 ♖d7 35 ♖c1 ♔e6 36 ♔e1 ½-½**

Often one would be tempted to play on with
rook and bishop vs rook and knight in an open
position. Here, however, Black is so well coor-
dinated (all of his pieces are outperforming
their counterparts) that any 'advantage' is purely
formal. Black himself can't make any winning
attempts without incurring significant risks, and
so a draw is a fair result.

Conclusions

1) In the line with 6 &c4 ♘b6 7 &b3, Black has two main options. The one he used in this game was the equalizing attempt 7...d5, and Black has no problems after this provided that he's well prepared. The theory in this line has been static for ages and never looked particularly promising for White in any event.

2) White's main attempts to pose problems for Black are based on the move ♘a3, either on move 9 or move 10. There are some subtleties in these endgames, and if Black doesn't know what he's doing he can get into trouble, but objectively there's nothing there.

3) If Black wants to avoid a draw, he can't do so without quite a lot of risk. In the first instance, I'd recommend 7...g6, but if you have to play 7...d5, then 13...♕c6 is a good attempt to deviate. However, after 14 ♖e1, 14...f6 is an extremely risky decision which, notwithstanding my praise of Mikhalevski's gumption, is probably just a mistake. 14...e6 and the game goes on.

Game 7
Sergei Zhigalko – Ildar Khairullin
World U-14 Ch, Kallithea 2003

1 e4 c5 2 c3 ♘f6 3 e5 ♘d5 4 ♘f3

The move-order 4 d4 cxd4 5 ♘f3 ♘c6 6 &c4 ♘b6 7 &b3 g6 is an alternative (and maybe more common) way to reach the position in the next diagram.

4...♘c6 5 &c4 ♘b6 6 &b3 g6

The continuations after 6...d5 or 6...d6 can be pretty drawish, as we saw in the previous game. Therefore Black has turned to alternative developments, and 6...g6 (or 7...g6) has proved to be an excellent choice for strong players who wish to play for a win. Throughout the c3 Sicilian, in fact, Black has been turning to a kingside fianchetto to unbalance several positions, and so far he has had reasonable success with this approach.

7 d4 cxd4 *(D)*

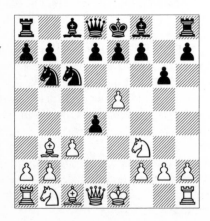

This is a difficult line for both players, and definitely needs some good preparation from Black. It is the subject of two games in this book. In this one, I look at the sharp 8 ♘g5!?, creating quick play against the f7-pawn. Game 8 is devoted to the underrated 8 cxd4, which leads to a structure typical of several variations in the c3 Sicilian.

8 ♘g5!?

This is perhaps critical – certainly, theory has regarded it as such, and due to the sharpness of the forthcoming variations, any player wanting to play 6...g6 would need to spend a lot of time on this line.

8...d5!

The main move, probably because it's the only one which leaves Black with a remotely playable position.

8...e6 9 ♘e4 leaves Black in a miserable position due to the weakness of his dark squares.

Nunn gives 8...♘xe5 9 &f4 ♘ec4 10 &xc4 ♘xc4 11 ♕xd4 f6 12 ♕xc4 fxg5 13 &e5! as excellent for White. Black needn't drop a whole rook as he can play 13...d5, but his position is horrible in any case.

9 exd6

If White doesn't take, his knight will look ridiculous on g5. He has to re-establish the threat against the f7-pawn.

9...e6 *(D)*

Now Black is preparing to take the d6-pawn.

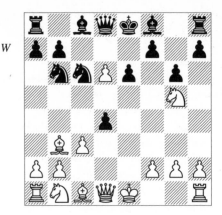

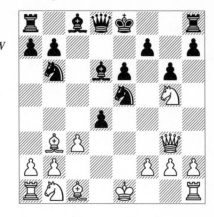

10 ♕f3

Continuing to play with short sharp threats.

10 ♘e4 poses few problems for Black – he can take on d6, play the main move 10...h6 or go with Nunn's suggested 10...♗g7!?, with the aim of recapturing the pawn later.

10...♘e5

Combining defence of f7 with an attack on the white queen.

10...f5!? is an interesting alternative; after 11 ♗xe6 ♗xe6 12 ♘xe6 ♕xd6 13 ♘xd4 ♘xd4 14 cxd4 ♕d5! Black has full positional compensation for his pawn deficit.

11 ♕g3

This is the best-established move.

11 ♕e4 is generally met by 11...♗g7: 12 cxd4 ♘ec4 13 ♘f3 ♘xd6 and I think Black is fine.

11 ♕h3 ♗g7 12 0-0 h6 13 ♘e4 also seems OK for Black after 13...♘ec4! and ...♘xd6.

11...♗xd6!? *(D)*

Original play. 11...♗g7 is more popular, with the aim of later playing ...♕xd6. White has never really managed to trouble Black here.

12 ♘e4

A natural move, centralizing the knight, hitting the d6-bishop and preparing ♗g5 or ♗h6.

12 0-0 ♘c6 13 ♗f4 ♗xf4 14 ♕xf4 0-0 has been played before, and looks a little better for White after 15 ♖d1.

12...♘ec4 13 ♕d3 ♘e5 14 ♕g3 ♘ec4 15 ♕d3 ♘e5 16 ♕xd4

White has every reason to play on, though I haven't managed to find any major improvements on the rest of the game – a remarkable

feat for a couple of 13-year-olds who were improvising.

16...♗c7 17 ♗g5!?

Playing for the initiative. 17 ♕xd8+ ♗xd8 18 ♗e3 is a quieter attempt – I don't think Black should really be worse here.

17...♕xd4 18 cxd4

Black is now faced with a tricky decision.

18...♘c6!

I think this is correct. 18...♘d3+?! 19 ♔e2 ♘f4+ (19...♘xb2? loses to 20 ♖c1 ♗d8 21 ♘d6+ ♔d7 22 ♘xf7 ♗xg5 23 ♘xg5, amongst others) 20 ♔f3 ♘fd5 21 ♘bc3 is good for White, whose pieces coordinate very effectively.

19 ♘f6+ ♔f8 20 ♗h6+ ♔e7 21 ♗g7 ♖d8 22 ♘xh7 *(D)*

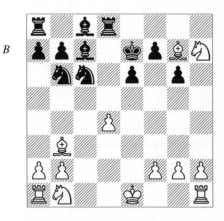

An unusual but effective way to win a pawn. The white pieces look ridiculous in the top right corner, but they combine to threaten ♗f6+.

22...♘d7!

By covering the f6-square, Black threatens ...♖g8 followed by ...♘xd4.

23 d5 ♗e5!

One of several good routes to equality.

24 ♗xe5 ♘cxe5 25 dxe6 ♘d3+ 26 ♔e2 ♘f4+ 27 ♔e3

This could be White's first mistake. 27 ♔f3 keeps the game alive: after 27...♘xe6 28 ♘c3 White plans ♘d5+ and ♘hf6, bringing the horse back into play. I'm not sure that Black has full compensation here.

27...♘xg2+ 28 ♔f3 ♘h4+ 29 ♔g4 ♘c5!

This could be what White missed – taking the h4-knight drops the one on h7.

30 ♔xh4 ♖h8 31 exf7 ½-½

I think we could be hearing more of these two players.

Conclusions

1) If Black wants to create winning chances in these ...♘c6 lines, ...g6 is a good way to do so. That said, he needs to do his homework before the game and make good moves during it, so it's not everyone's cup of tea.

2) 8 ♘g5 is a very aggressive option which leaves quite a lot of scope for original and creative play. This game is an excellent example of this. If you feel capable of outplaying your opponent in an unbalanced struggle, this is the move for you.

Game 8
Vladimir Baklan – Alfonso Romero Holmes
Bled Olympiad 2002

1 e4 c5 2 c3 ♘f6 3 e5 ♘d5 4 ♘f3 ♘c6 5 ♗c4 ♘b6 6 ♗b3 g6!? 7 d4 cxd4 8 cxd4 *(D)*

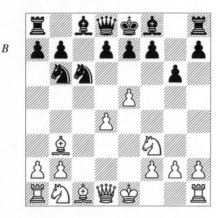

This simple recapture is very far from stupid. In fact, I think Black has some problems here, and GM Joel Benjamin agrees.

8...♗g7

If Black wants to avoid the pawn sacrifice at move 9, he can try either 8...d5 or 8...d6, though it should be said that, objectively speaking, it is nothing to fear.

Now White has two major options.

9 ♘c3

This move is very natural. 9 d5!? is an enterprising alternative, sacrificing the e5-pawn in order to keep Black's king in the centre. After 9...♘xe5 10 ♘xe5 ♗xe5 11 ♗h6 e6 (Finkel gives 11...♗xb2 12 ♘d2 ♗xa1 13 ♕xa1 f6 14 d6! with a strong attack) 12 ♘c3 ♕h4 13 ♕d2 White has some initiative.

9...0-0 10 0-0 *(D)*

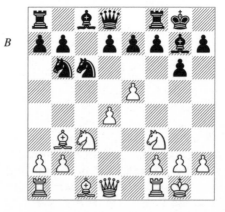

Black now needs to decide how to challenge the white centre. There are two main approaches – in this game, I think Black opts for the wrong one, but White's treatment is very instructive so

I've included it on that basis. 8 cxd4 is generally perceived as innocuous, but I don't see the reason for this view – Black faces some unpleasant problems in several lines.

10...d5

I think this game constitutes a rather strong argument against this move. With the bishop on e7, a black pawn on d5 is fine. After a kingside fianchetto, however, Black needs to start breaking down the white centre so that the g7-bishop can breathe. I would have preferred to aim for ...d6, rather than ...f6 as is played in the game.

10...d6 has led to some problems for Black recently, even though it must be the best move. Nunn writes that "the position is roughly equal. Black is already exerting strong pressure against e5, which he can step up by ...♗g4. If White cannot maintain his e5-pawn, then he is unlikely to gain any worthwhile advantage." In practice White has done better than this assessment would suggest; in the two games which follow after 11 exd6 *(D)*, Black failed to neutralize White's initiative:

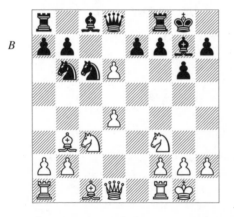

a) 11...♕xd6 (this virtually compels White to sacrifice the d4-pawn) 12 ♘b5!? ♕d8 13 h3 a6 14 ♘c3 ♘xd4 15 ♘xd4 ♕xd4 16 ♕e2 e6 17 ♗e3 ♕b4 18 ♖fd1 ♘d7 19 ♖ac1 ♘e5?! (19...♕h4 is a tighter defence, but I think White has interesting compensation in any event) 20 ♘a4! ♕h4? 21 ♘b6 ♖b8 22 ♗c5 ♘c6 23 ♗xf8 ♗xf8 24 ♗a4 ♕b4 25 ♗xc6 ♕xb6 26 ♗f3 1-0 Paragua-Kalygin, Alushta 2004.

b) 11...♗g4 is a clever move: 12 dxe7 ♕xe7 13 ♗e3 ♗xf3?! (Nunn indicates 13...♗xd4! 14

♗xd4 ♗xf3 15 ♕xf3 ♘xd4, equalizing) 14 ♕xf3 ♘xd4 15 ♗xd4 ♗xd4 16 ♖ad1 (Black is a whisker away from equality, but the white pressure down the central files proves annoying enough to create some problems) 16...♗g7 17 ♖fe1 ♕c7 18 ♘b5 ♕c5 19 ♘d6 ♕c7 20 ♕xb7 ♕xb7 21 ♘xb7 a5 22 a4 ♗xb2 23 ♖e7 and White had an enduring initiative in the endgame of T.Kosintseva-Balabaev, Russia Cup (rapid Internet qualifier) 2004. The opposite-coloured bishops are not of enormous relevance here, since both sides each have three other pieces.

11 h3

An important move – ...♗g4 would have created useful pressure on d4 as well as developing the remaining black minor piece. Black now has some problems with his queen's bishop. It can go to f5, but seems something of a target here (White has options like ♘h4 or ♘e2-g3).

Of course, 11 exd6 transposes to the previous note.

11...f6

This is necessary at some point over the next few moves, and there's no real reason to delay.

12 exf6

Allowing Black to take on e5 and then block with ...e6 would be a clear strategic error, since the only weak pawn in the position would be White's one on e5.

12...exf6 *(D)*

Black has to recapture with the pawn in order to retain control of the important e5- and g5-squares.

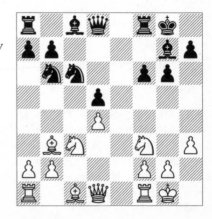

In my view, White has a small but enduring advantage. The position is nearly symmetrical, but with a couple of important differences:

1) Black's kingside structure is loose.

2) The white knights are ideally placed, while the black steed on b6 is a poor piece.

13 ♖e1

Playing a rook to the open file like this is always a good idea, especially when Black can't respond in kind since 13...♖e8? drops the d-pawn after 14 ♖xe8+ ♕xe8 15 ♘xd5.

After something like 13 ♗f4 Black has one extra option compared to the game – I'm not sure if it's best but it's definitely worth stopping: 13...♗e6 followed by ...♗f7 shoring up the d-pawn and the weak a2-g8 diagonal.

13...♘a5

This knight manoeuvre seems to lose some time, but in fact it's quite smart to kick the white bishop off the a2-g8 diagonal.

14 ♗c2

The bishop is important and has to be retained.

14...♘ac4?!

This creates too much of a target. Simple development with 14...♗d7 is preferable.

15 a4! (D)

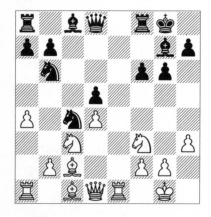

A typical way to play against the b6-knight. It would be uncomfortable to allow a5 (especially since White can play it whenever he wants), while blocking the pawn (as in the game) leaves the b5-square as a more relevant weakness than the b4-square.

15...a5

An essential move at some point. After 15...♘a5 16 ♗f4 ♘c6 17 b3, for instance, Black will need to block the a-pawn since the perpetual threat of a5 is unbearable.

16 b3

This move takes away the b3-square from the light-squared bishop, but allows the other prelate to come into play.

16...♘d6 17 ♗a3!

Much better than something like 17 ♗f4 – now both knights will be hit after 18 ♗c5.

17...♖f7

This is extremely passive. The idea is to unpin the d6-knight so that ...♗f5 is an option, but this plan is just too slow. Challenging for the e-file with 17...♖e8 is more logical, when White is 'only' clearly better following 18 ♖xe8+ ♘xe8 19 ♕d2 ♘c7 20 ♖e1.

18 ♗c5! (D)

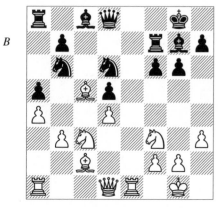

The knight on b6 is a miserable piece, but it's the only thing holding the d-pawn.

18...♗f5

Black might as well get the bishops off. After 18...♗f8 White can consider ignoring the pawn and maintaining a bind; for instance, 19 ♕d2 ♗d7 20 ♖ac1 ♗c6 21 ♕f4 followed by ♗d3 and ♖e6 with absolute domination.

19 ♗xb6

It was possible to wait, as in the last note, but a pawn's a pawn.

19...♕xb6 20 ♘xd5

White wins material and retains the better position.

20...♕c6

After 20...♕d8 21 ♗xf5 ♘xf5, the plan of invading on e6 with 22 ♘f4! becomes more attractive because the knight will gain a tempo on the black queen.

21 ♗xf5 ♘xf5 22 ♘e3!

22 ♘f4, aiming for the e6-square, is an alternative plan, but there's no need for this – simply exchanging the only good black piece is enough to win without any counterplay.

22...♘xe3

Black drags a white rook to e3 so that ...♗h6 will gain a tempo. 22...♕d7 23 ♘xf5 ♕xf5 24 ♖c1 leaves White with both files and a simple win.

23 ♖xe3 *(D)*

23 fxe3?! is manifestly the wrong idea – White shouldn't weaken his king, especially when the d-pawn will soon prove untouchable.

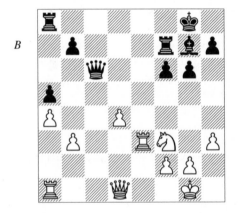

23...♗h6

Consistent.

24 d5

White doesn't have to do this, but it's nice to get as much of the position onto light squares as possible.

24...♕c5

This is the best available square for Black's queen.

25 ♖d3 ♖d8

25...♖e8 26 ♖a2 ♖fe7 at least makes a pretence at activity, though White is still dominant.

26 ♖a2!

Since c1 is not available, the rook aims for c2.

26...♕c1?

This really doesn't help – now White need never fear an attack on his king. I think Black needed to keep as many pieces on as possible, so as to retain swindling chances.

27 ♕xc1 ♗xc1 28 ♖c2

Gaining time on the bishop.

28...♗a3

At least this diagonal is quite useful, but by abandoning control of d2 Black allows the white knight into a sweet outpost.

29 ♘d2! ♗b4 30 ♘c4 ♖fd7 *(D)*

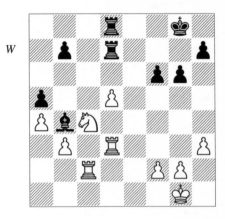

Just for a moment it appears that Black has created some real pressure on d5, but the forthcoming exchange further reduces his prospects.

31 ♘b6! ♖d6

31...♖e7 might be slightly more precise, since 32 ♖c8 ♖xc8 33 ♘xc8 ♖e1+ 34 ♔h2 ♔f7 gives Black a better defensive set-up than in the game. If White is feeling sadistic, 32 g3! is the way to avoid even this degree of counterplay.

32 ♖c8 ♖xc8 33 ♘xc8 ♖d8 34 ♘b6 ♗c5 35 ♘c4 b6

This endgame is an absolute dream for White. The only question is whether he can break through – and that's not such a difficult question.

36 g4!

Opening a route for the king, gaining space and fixing the black f6-pawn.

36...♔f7 37 ♔g2 ♖e8 38 ♔f1 ♖e4

The rook is well placed here, but the lack of white weaknesses is very significant.

39 ♖d2!?

So that he can challenge on the e-file – also, ...♖f4 won't come with tempo (though that would have been a rather dubious idea anyway).

39...♖e8 40 ♖d1 ♖e4 41 ♖d2

Repeating moves is a common ploy in such endgames – nothing is risked (provided you don't repeat twice, and get the same position three times!) and the opponent may lose his composure and play an inferior continuation. It helps avoid time-trouble too.

41...♖e8 42 ♖c2

Setting up an attack on the black bishop.

42...♖a8 43 ♔g2 ♖d8

Provoking White into the forthcoming exchange. I think this is a sensible approach by Black, since the passed d-pawn is probably more valuable than the black a-pawn.

44 ♘xa5!?

Transforming the advantage – White didn't have to do this, but I think it's a reasonable idea.

44...♖xd5

Notwithstanding that 'all rook endgames are drawn', 44...bxa5? 45 ♖xc5 really is hopeless, especially in view of 45...♖b8 46 ♖b5, when the black rook is forced into passivity in order to hang on to at least some of his pawns.

45 ♘b7 *(D)*

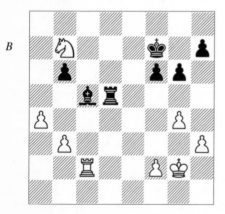

The knight hits some key squares and supports a queenside advance, though it's always a little risky to play one's horses into the corners.

45...♔e6?

I think Black overlooked White's threat. 45...♗d4 is a tougher defence, though 46 ♖c7+ looks strong.

46 a5!

White exploits the position of the c5-bishop to advance his a-pawn.

46...♗d4 47 a6

Queening is now a real possibility.

47...b5

This is forced in order to cover the pawn, but now the knight can slip out.

48 ♘a5 ♖d7 49 ♘c6

An amazing square for the knight, paralysing the whole black position.

49...♗a7 50 b4 ♔d6 51 ♘a5 ♖c7 52 ♘b7+ ♔d7 53 ♖d2+ ♔e7 54 ♘a5 ♗b6 55 ♖d5!

The beginning of the end.

55...♗xa5 56 ♖xb5!

A cute trick. 56 bxa5 ♖a7 57 ♖xb5 ♖xa6 would have been much trickier. The active position of the white rook coupled with the continuing weakness of f6 provide good chances, but I'm far from sure that this is a forced win.

56...♗xb4 57 ♖xb4

While normally playing the rook behind the passed pawn is enough to win such positions, here there are tactical features which mean that even this plan is unnecessary.

57...♔d8

There's nothing better, since 57...♖a7 loses to 58 ♖b7+.

58 ♖b6 1-0

Totally decisive: 58...♔e7 59 ♖b7 and 60 a7 would end matters.

Conclusions

1) 8 cxd4 is a nasty line for Black to face. One of the reasons is that he needs to spend so much time learning the lines after 8 ♘g5, that he will very probably have given White's quieter 8th-move alternatives little more than a cursory glance.

2) The pawn sacrifice at move 9 is a nice option for White to have, though I think it's more trouble than it's worth. He gives up a big central pawn and cuts his options down considerably.

3) At move 10, Black should hit the e5-pawn rather than leave it. If you're preparing this line with White, 10...d6 is the main move to look at. That said, our main game here is an excellent example of how to handle a typical c3 Sicilian structure.

Game 9
Andrei Deviatkin – Bartlomiej Macieja
Rapidplay, Warsaw 2005

1 e4 c5 2 c3 ♘f6 3 e5 ♘d5 4 d4 cxd4 5 ♕xd4 *(D)*

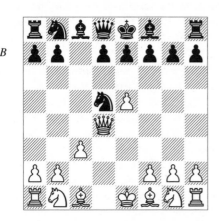

This has never really caught on, though many good players have essayed it on occasion. Original thinkers such as GMs Ian Rogers, Evgeny Sveshnikov and Eduardas Rozentalis have each played several games here, with varied success. White isn't really aiming for an opening advantage, just an original position from which he can outplay his opponent.

5...e6

Supporting the knight like this is pretty automatic. 5...♘b6 might also be playable, with some similar themes to the Alekhine Defence.

6 ♘f3

6 ♗c4 is the alternative. After 6...♘c6 7 ♕e4, the queen can drop back to e2 if Black hits with 7...f5 (and the light-squared bishop won't complain this time, since it's already developed). 7...d6 is more logical, when an equal endgame was reached after 8 ♘f3 dxe5 9 ♘xe5 ♘f6 10 ♘xc6 ♘xe4 11 ♘xd8 ♔xd8 12 ♗e3 ♗c5 13 ♔e2 ♗xe3 14 ♔xe3 ♘d6 in Striković-Shirov, Bilbao (rapid) 2001.

6...♘c6

Black has also played the immediate 6...d6, but it makes sense to gain time on the queen.

7 ♕e4 *(D)*

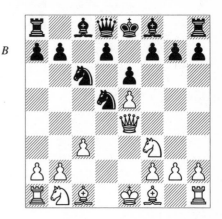

The queen is well placed in the centre, but Black can exploit the lack of pawn-support for the e5-strongpoint.

7...d6

Hitting e5 like this is extremely logical.

7...f5 is more ambitious. 8 ♕e2 (8 exf6 ♘xf6 is quite comfortable for Black, who has a 2-0 advantage in central pawns) 8...♕c7 9 g3 b5!? 10 ♗g2 (10 ♕xb5 ♘xe5 is good for Black) 10...a5 11 0-0 ♗a6 and Black has an active game with reasonable chances in an unclear position – a successful opening outcome.

8 ♗b5

Pinning the knight and preparing to get the king out of the centre.

8 ♘bd2 is the main move, but in such lines the 'main moves' never lead to anything substantial. Here, Black has a simple and reliable response: 8...dxe5 9 ♘xe5 ♘xe5 10 ♕xe5. The queen is White's only good piece, so Black offers an exchange with 10...♕c7! and now 11 ♗b5+ ♗d7 12 ♗xd7+ ♕xd7 followed by ...♕c7! leaves White with no advantage.

8...♗d7

This isn't strictly necessary, but is certainly the most consistent – Black breaks the pin, develops and re-establishes the threat of mass simplification on e5.

9 c4

This is an interesting attempt to trouble Black, but Macieja retains his composure.

9...♘c7 *(D)*

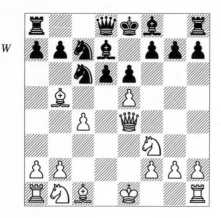

10 ♗g5

It looks very logical to attack the black queen while developing, but Macieja finds an excellent response.

The immediate 10 exd6 ♗xd6 11 0-0 merits testing.

10...♕b8!

The queen looks clumsy here, but is actually well placed on the b8-h2 diagonal. Instead, 10...♗e7 is impossible in view of 11 exd6, while 10...f6 weakens the black structure unnecessarily.

11 exd6

The latent pressure on the e5-pawn encourages this capture.

11 ♗f4 d5! 12 ♕e2 ♘xb5 13 cxb5 ♘e7 followed by ...♘g6 leaves Black with a very comfortable game.

11...♗xd6 12 ♘c3 ♘xb5

12...0-0? 13 0-0-0! lands Black in major trouble because of the targets on the d-file.

13 cxb5

Hitting the knight gains time, but this is still a significant weakening of White's pawn-structure.

13 ♘xb5 ♗b4+ is fine for Black since White has no constructive way to deal with the check.

13...♘e5 14 0-0-0!?

Pretty aggressive, but I think this is what the position requires. Quieter play would give Black good chances to consolidate.

White had an interesting pawn sacrifice at his disposal: 14 0-0, when 14...♘xf3+ 15 ♕xf3 ♗xh2+ 16 ♔h1 ♗e5 17 ♖fd1 gives him good compensation. I think Black is well advised to avoid this with, for instance, 14...f6!?.

14...♘xf3 15 ♕xf3 f6!

This is very precise. 15...0-0 16 ♕d3 ♗f4+ 17 ♗xf4 ♕xf4+ 18 ♕d2 ♕xd2+ 19 ♖xd2 gives White a better version of the endgame, since the black king is stuck in the corner and the d7-bishop is passive.

16 ♕d3

This more or less forces a draw, as the resulting endgame doesn't promise much at all for White, but other continuations leave him in danger of being worse; for instance, 16 ♗e3 ♕c7 17 ♔b1 0-0, when Black has two bishops and the better structure.

16...fxg5 17 ♕xd6 ♕xd6 18 ♖xd6 ♔e7

It seems that the weaknesses on b5 and g5 cancel each other out, as instanced by the game continuation.

19 ♖hd1 ♗e8 20 ♖6d4 ♖c8 21 ♖e1 ♗xb5
½-½

Playing a rook to the fifth rank will regain the pawn. This is a very interesting game for such a short draw in a rapidplay event, and is an important development in the theory of 5 ♕xd4.

Conclusions

1) I think offbeat lines can be divided into three categories – those which contain tactical traps; those which can give a slight advantage against imperfect defence; and those which are solely played to get out of the book. 5 ♕xd4, in my opinion, falls squarely into the third category. The move doesn't have any real ideas behind it, but does avoid the 'bulk' of c3 Sicilian theory. There isn't too much c3 Sicilian theory, but this avoids it anyway.

2) After 6 ♗c4, it's important to remember that defences with ...f5 basically don't work. Play ...d6 and equalize.

3) After 6 ♘f3 ♘c6 7 ♕e4, Black has a choice to make. I think 7...f5 is well worth a look. 7...d6 leaves White with some options, but Black has nothing to worry about from a theoretical point of view.

3   2...♘f6: White Avoids an Early d4

1 e4 c5 2 c3 ♘f6 3 e5 ♘d5

In recent years, attention has turned away from systems with 4 d4 to those where White delays this move, or even avoids it altogether. This trend can be attributed to two factors. The first (subjective) factor is that, as people get bored of playing the same lines where Black has several routes to an acceptable position, a desire for innovation is natural and so people start looking for different possibilities. The second (objective) factor is that Black has not yet completely neutralized these new systems, and so it could be that delaying d4 is the 'best' way to play the c3 Sicilian.

4 ♘f3

Of course White can still play d4 later, but he's trying to sound out what Black is up to.

4 ♗c4 is the latest attempt to avoid the main lines. See Game 12, Tiviakov-Parligas, for the details.

4...♘c6

The most flexible response, since this knight is rarely deployed to another square. In this chapter, we look at White's attempt to keep the game in independent channels:

5 ♗c4 ♘b6 6 ♗b3

Now Black has a basic choice – try to transpose back to the 4 d4 lines, or seek to exploit White's omission. As is generally the case in chess, the more ambitious option seems to be better.

6...d5 is a tacit request to get back to the 4 d4 lines, but White has promising alternatives. Game 10, Tiviakov-Carlsen, shows how tricky it can be for Black to bring his position to safety.

6...c4 pushes the bishop back and significantly weakens the e5-pawn. Game 11, Pavasović-Epishin, is an instructive encounter in this line between two theoretical experts.

Game 10
Sergei Tiviakov – Magnus Carlsen
Gausdal 2005

Magnus Carlsen is one of the outstanding talents of his generation, with superb imagination and attacking instincts. He doesn't get to show any of these qualities after landing in a dismal c3 Sicilian endgame.

1 e4 c5 2 c3 ♘f6 3 e5 ♘d5 4 ♘f3 ♘c6 5 ♗c4 ♘b6 6 ♗b3 d5

This move, which is a clean equalizer in the analogous line 5 d4 cxd4 6 ♗c4 ♘b6 7 ♗b3 d5!, hasn't been performing so well in this particular position. White has some very useful options based on delaying or avoiding both 0-0 and d4.

7 exd6 (D)

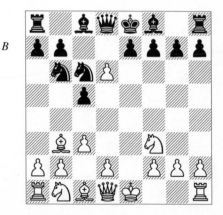

The d5-pawn had to go.

7...♕xd6

This is Black's last chance to deviate, and personally I think he should take it. 7...c4 8 ♗c2 transposes to the note Black's 7th move in Game 11.

8 ♘a3!

This is the point. Playing the knight to a3 is much more flexible than either 0-0 or d4 (since it can be followed by either of these moves).

8...e6

This reply is passive and, while solid, still requires some good theoretical knowledge on Black's part.

8...♗e6 is the main alternative. After 9 d4 ♗xb3 10 ♕xb3 cxd4 11 ♘b5 ♕b8, in Tiviakov-Külaots, Gausdal 2005, White introduced an important novelty: 12 g3!?. After 12...♕d8 (Tiviakov suggests 12...dxc3 13 ♗f4 cxb2 14 ♕xb2 e5 15 ♘xe5 ♘xe5 16 ♗xe5 ♘c4 17 ♗xb8 ♘xb2 18 ♗xa7 ♔d7, when White has some initiative after 19 0-0 but Black shouldn't lose) 13 ♗f4 ♖c8 14 0-0-0 Black was under pressure. The game is a model demonstration of how difficult such positions can be for Black – he gets into an endgame, but finds no salvation there: 14...♕d5 15 ♘fxd4 ♘xd4 16 ♘xd4 ♕xb3 17 axb3 e6 18 ♖he1 ♗c5 19 ♘b5! (this is often the move which puts Black on the ropes in a c3 Sicilian endgame; here, in addition to the usual pressure points on c7 and d6, the knight hits the a7-pawn and thus gains a useful tempo) 19...a6 20 ♘d6+ ♗xd6 21 ♖xd6 (an extra frustration for Black is that his knight is now unprotected) 21...♖c6 22 ♖xc6 bxc6 *(D)*.

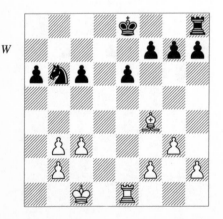

In purely static terms, Black's structure is not clearly worse than White's – he has two isolated pawns, but White has doubled pawns and a crippled majority. However, the a6- and c6-pawns are genuine targets, while the doubled pawn on b3 severely restricts the black knight. That said, White needs to play precisely in order to crystallize his advantage, and Tiviakov's next two moves are right on the money: 23 ♗e5! ♖g8 24 ♖e4! (preparing to swing the rook to the b-file) 24...♔e7 25 ♖b4 ♘d7 26 ♖b7 f6 27 ♗d4 ♖b8 28 ♖a7 ♖xb3 (this permits a simple refutation, but Black was busted in any event) 29 ♗c5+ ♔d8 30 ♗b4 (the rook is now incarcerated) 30...c5 31 ♔c2 c4 32 ♖xa6 ♘e5 33 ♖d6+ ♔c7 34 ♖d4 1-0. Black resigned since the c4-pawn falls, followed closely by the b3-rook.

8...a6 has also been tested. There can follow 9 0-0 ♗f5 10 d4 cxd4 11 ♘xd4 (the knight exchange allows the white queen to occupy a good square) 11...♘xd4 12 cxd4 e6 13 ♕f3 *(D)*, and now:

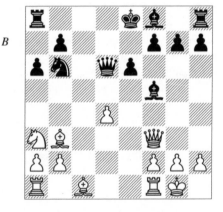

a) 13...♕c6?! 14 d5! ♘xd5 15 ♖d1 ♘b6 16 ♕g3 ♘d5 17 ♘c4 ♖d8 18 ♘e3 ♗g6 19 ♘xd5 exd5 20 ♗g5 was winning for White in Sermek-Kiseliov, Ljubljana 1992.

b) 13...♕d7 14 d5!? ♘xd5 15 ♖d1 (White has some initiative for his pawn) 15...♗xa3 (otherwise the knight comes to c4, but now White has the two bishops) 16 bxa3 0-0 17 h4 (threatening to trap the bishop with g4 and h5) 17...♖ac8 (preparing ...♗c2) occurred in Stevanović-Prevot, European Railways Ch, Dresden 2000. Okhotnik recommends 18 ♖d2, when

White has more than enough compensation for the pawn, since the two bishops will combine well with the queen and h-pawn to generate a kingside attack.

9 d4 *(D)*

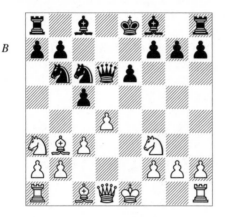

Now White has the option of dxc5 and (in some lines) ♗f4.

9...♗e7?!

The 'dubious' annotation is Tiviakov's, from his notes in *New in Chess Yearbook 78*. He suggests that 9...a6 is sufficient for equality, with the following indicative lines:

a) 10 0-0 cxd4 11 cxd4 ♗e7 is a line he gave as equal. The white knight is badly placed on a3 in such a structure – it would rather be on c3. Now its only developing options are:

• c4, where it can be exchanged for the b6-knight (exchanges generally favour the defender in IQP positions, because he has less space and would like to reduce his opponent's attacking chances);

• c2, from where its only forward option (to e3) would entomb the c1-bishop; or

• b1, aiming for the correct square (c3) at considerable loss of time – there's no way White could be better in such a situation.

b) 10 dxc5 ♕xd1+ 11 ♗xd1 ♗xc5 12 ♘c2 is another line he gave as equal. In such endgames, White needs a high level of technique to avoid becoming worse, because the pawn-structure is basically favourable for Black (he could gain central space by advancing his e- and f-pawns, while the advance of the white queenside majority shouldn't cause too many problems).

c) 10 ♗e3 cxd4 11 ♘xd4 ♘d5 is given by Tiviakov as unclear, but it seems to be White's best shot at an advantage. Continuing the analysis: 12 ♘c4 ♕c7 13 0-0 ♗d7 and now White has a choice of aggressive queen developments on the kingside; for instance, 14 ♕g4, when he has some initiative since the development of the f8-bishop is problematic.

Unfortunately, nobody has tried 9...a6 yet so we'll have to await future practical tests.

10 ♘b5! *(D)*

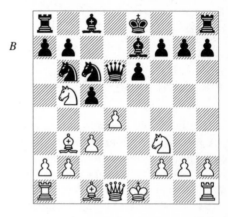

Naturally such a move must be well-calculated – you have to do something with the knight on b5 before it gets kicked. In this position, the move has two benefits:

1) Black's queen is forced to an inferior square;

2) White has a device to secure control of the d6-square.

10...♕d8?

After this, Black's defence becomes very difficult. Maybe Magnus didn't foresee the problems this endgame holds for Black.

Tiviakov gives 10...♕b8 as the 'only move', but White is still better; for instance, 11 dxc5 ♗xc5 12 ♗e3 ♗xe3 13 ♘d6+ ♔e7 14 ♘xc8+ ♖xc8 15 fxe3 with some initiative due to the awkward position of the black king, and the semi-open f-file which can be used for a kingside attack.

11 dxc5!

Black's pieces simply aren't ready for this opening of the position.

11...♗xc5

Black cannot contemplate 11...♕xd1+? 12 ♔xd1 since then both cxb6 and ♘c7+ are threatened.

12 ♕xd8+ ♔xd8 *(D)*

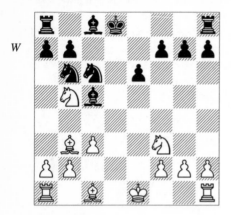

The fact that White was able to take on d8 (while Black couldn't afford to take on d1) is a significant factor in establishing White's advantage here. In similar endgames where White is forced to take on d1 with the king, he generally needs a substantial lead in development in order to claim an advantage. Here, however, the poor placement of the black king allows the white pieces to come into action with tempo. I'll also draw your attention to the black knights, which can simply be worked around – the one on b6 has no identifiable function (control of d7, perhaps?) and while the c6-knight prevents ♘e5, the f3-knight has a perfectly good alternative in ♘g5.

13 ♗f4 a6

Given that the knight can go forward, this move doesn't seem to help Black's cause. However, he doesn't have anything better – the multiple threats of bringing a knight (or bishop) to c7 (or d6) are too strong as a collective, and so must be crystallized into one move – it's better to force White to make one strong move immediately rather than have four threats hanging indefinitely.

14 ♖d1+ ♗d7?!

Tiviakov suggests 14...♔e7 15 ♘c7 (or 15 ♘d6) 15...♖a7 16 ♘g5 ♘a8 17 ♘e4 ♘xc7 18 ♘xc5, when White is clearly better, but not yet winning.

15 ♘c7! ♖c8 16 ♘g5!

The two knight jumps have placed Black in a critical position.

16...e5 17 ♘d5 ♘xd5

If 17...exf4 18 ♘xf7+ ♔e8 19 ♘xb6 ♗xb6 20 ♘xh8 the knight escapes via f7, leaving White with an overwhelming material advantage.

18 ♘xf7+ ♔e7 19 ♖xd5

19 ♘xh8?? isn't too smart in view of the reply 19...♘xf4.

19...exf4 *(D)*

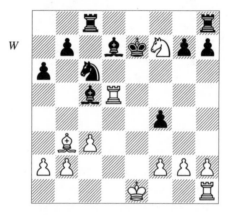

20 ♖xc5?!

This is inaccurate, though the resulting endgame is instructive and quite typical.

Tiviakov's analysis shows that 20 ♘xh8 would have won on the spot:

a) 20...♗b6 21 0-0 ♖xh8 22 ♖e1+ ♔d8 23 ♖ed1 ♘b8 24 ♗a4 and White wins a piece.

b) 20...b6 21 0-0 ♖xh8 22 ♖e1+ ♔d8 23 ♖ed1 ♘b8 24 ♗a4 b5 25 ♗c2 threatens ♗f5.

c) 20...♘a5 21 ♗d1 intending ♖xd7+ and ♗g4+.

20...♖hf8 21 ♘g5

21 ♘e5 is a good alternative.

21...♖f5

This is an interesting decision by Carlsen – in principle, exchanges favour White, but the rook on c5 is extremely active. I think he hoped to make something of his superior development, but as it turns out, Tiviakov is able to cover everything. However, 21...h6 22 ♘f3 ♗g4 looks like a better attempt.

22 ♖xf5 ♗xf5 23 0-0

Another interesting decision – the king tends to be well placed in the centre in such simplified positions, but Tiviakov wants to leave the central files open for his rook. A contest between the rooks for control of these lines would be no bad thing, since it is likely to lead to their exchange, and then the white king will be able to come out.

23...♔f6 24 ♘f3 *(D)*

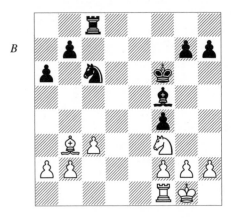

It's definitely too early to speak of a 'won game', but White has excellent winning prospects. In general, the old adage holds true here – White, with a material advantage, wants to exchange pieces; Black, a pawn down, wants to exchange pawns. This rule should be fleshed out a little. Though White would welcome a rook exchange and a knight exchange (also a bishop exchange, provided the activity of the black king and knight in the resulting endgame didn't prove sufficient to regain the pawn), he shouldn't exchange dissimilar pieces, i.e. knight for bishop or vice versa. Vishy Anand pointed out that such exchanges have the effect of increasing the defending side's drawing chances in such positions. I'm not sure how to rationalize the rule, but I have faith in Vishy!

24...♖e8 25 ♖d1 ♖e2 26 ♖d6+!

Getting the black king to plug the e-file.

26...♔e7 27 ♖d2 ♖xd2 28 ♘xd2

Good news for White, but this is one of the advantages of having extra material – if a rook exchange is favourable for White, then by definition the black rook can never get truly active, since it would need to run away whenever it

faced the white rook. Of course, Black had no choice but to exchange rooks here.

28...♘e5 29 g3

In general, White will avoid pawn exchanges, but the creation of a potential weakness on f4 is too good to pass up.

29...g5 30 gxf4 gxf4 31 ♗d5 b6

A world-class grandmaster like Carlsen is obviously reluctant to put his pawns on the same colour squares as his bishop.

32 ♔g2 ♗g4 33 b4 ♔d6 34 ♗e4 h6 35 ♘f3 *(D)*

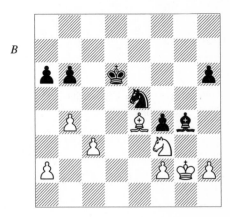

35...♘xf3

In view of Anand's comment (see the note to move 24), Black could have considered 35...♗xf3+ here, but after 36 ♗xf3 I think the white bishop is just too strong – it also coordinates very effectively with the white pawns, since they've been placed on dark squares.

36 ♗xf3 ♗e6 37 a3 ♔e5

Tiviakov's technique is excellent. First, he improves his king and bishop:

38 ♗b7 a5 39 ♔f3 ♗d7 40 ♗e4 ♗a4 41 ♗d3 ♗d7 42 ♗f1 ♗e6 43 ♗b5 ♗f5 44 ♔e2 ♗e4 45 ♔d2 ♗f5 46 ♗d3 ♗e6 47 ♔c2 ♗f7 48 ♗f1 ♗e6 49 ♔d3 ♗f7

Obviously the king can't be hit: 49...♗f5+ 50 ♔c4 axb4 (50...♗d7 51 bxa5 bxa5 52 ♔c5 wins for White) 51 cxb4!? and a passed pawn on the a-file will be hard to stop.

Now, White pushes the c-pawn.

50 c4 axb4

I guess the reason Magnus delayed this capture was to prevent White from taking with the c-pawn and creating a passed a-pawn (as indicated in the note to Black's 49th).

51 axb4 ♗g6+ 52 ♔c3 ♗e4 53 c5! *(D)*

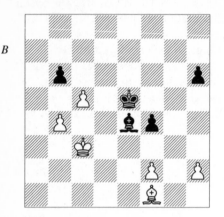

B

Simply winning – there's no defence to the white king's invasion.

53...bxc5 54 bxc5 ♗c6 55 ♔b4 ♗d5 56 ♔b5 ♔e4 57 ♗e2 f3 58 ♗c4 ♗a8 59 c6 ♔d4 60 c7 ♗b7 61 ♗e6 1-0

Rather than 62 c8♕, the real threat is 62 ♔b6.

Conclusions

1) The fact that Magnus Carlsen didn't manage to get out of the opening with a playable position is indicative of the poison contained in these systems where White delays d4.

2) 6...d5 is a difficult move to recommend. If Black really knows his stuff, he might make it to a level endgame; however, there are plenty of traps to navigate along the way.

3) 8...♗e6 looks a little more active than 8...e6.

4) Tiviakov's suggestion of 9...a6 is clearly the way to play with Black.

5) This game is a good illustration of how difficult these endgames can be for Black.

Game 11

Duško Pavasović – Vladimir Epishin
Nova Gorica 2006

1 e4 c5 2 c3 ♘f6 3 e5 ♘d5 4 ♘f3 ♘c6 5 ♗c4 ♘b6 6 ♗b3 c4

We saw in the last game that 6...d5 is no bed of roses for Black. With 6...c4, Epishin exploits the fact that the white d-pawn is still at home – now d4 can always be met by an *en passant* capture, which means that the e5-pawn is denied its most natural support.

7 ♗c2 *(D)*

The most important factor in this position is the relative weakness of the pawns on c4 and e5.

7...♕c7

Black plays consistently to undermine and attack the e5-pawn, a theme which is continued by his next two moves.

7...d6 is also an important line. Pavasović faced it twice in 2005, winning against Beliavsky and losing to Wells, but these stats are misleading because he was winning in both games. 8 exd6 ♕xd6 9 0-0 is the natural continuation. White is now preparing to get rid of

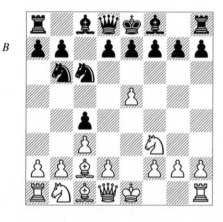

B

the cramping c4-pawn by playing b3, and then seize the centre with d4. Black now has:

a) 9...g6 10 ♘a3 ♗g7 11 b3 cxb3 12 axb3 0-0 13 d4 ♗g4 is a good option – Black prepares to strike in the middle with ...e5. I also like the fact that he heads to the kingside – the queenside looks pretty fragile, since the c4-pawn makes it easy to prise things open with b3.

b) 9...♗g4 10 ♖e1 *(D)* is a position which seems absolutely fine for Black on the surface, but in fact I think he has some problems here.

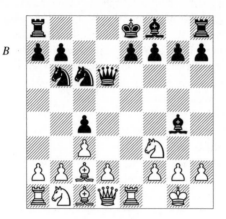

Neither Beliavsky nor Wells, both strong theoreticians, got out of the opening with a playable position:

b1) 10...♕f6 seems to put pressure on the f3-knight, but after 11 b3 it becomes apparent that this is an empty threat – Black won't take twice on f3 because the white bishop will be dominant on e4 in an endgame. 11...e6 12 ♗e4 0-0-0 13 ♕e2 ♗d6 14 bxc4 ♗xf3 15 ♗xf3 ♕f4 16 g3 ♕xc4 (Beliavsky's simple tactics have regained the pawn, but with the two bishops White has a very pleasant advantage) 17 d3 ♕a6 18 ♗xc6 bxc6 (the open b-file makes the black king uneasy) 19 ♗g5 ♖d7 20 ♘d2 ♗c7 21 c4 h6 22 ♗e3 ♖hd8 23 ♘b3 ♘a4 24 d4 and White dominated in Pavasović-Beliavsky, Vidmar Memorial, Portorož 2005.

b2) With 10...♘e5, Black exploits the pin on the f3-knight to force an exchange. White replies with 11 ♖xe5 ♗xf3 12 ♕e1!. The past couple of moves have seen a knight exchange, even if it was in a non-standard fashion. Black now has to withdraw his bishop, leaving White with another tempo for development. The white queen and rook aren't badly placed on the e-file. The black knight had moved twice, the white one only once. In short, it's hard to see what Black has gained by this exchanging operation, and I think it can be classed as a mistake. 12...♗d5 13 b3! (the correct way to hit the c-pawn – White opens the b-file and prepares

♗a3, while the d-pawn is left to cover the central squares) 13...e6 14 ♗a3 ♕c6 15 ♖g5! (now, instead of generating a kingside attack, Black will have kingside weaknesses to attend to) 15...f6 16 ♖g3 0-0-0 17 ♗xf8 ♖hxf8 18 ♘a3! (naturally, 18 ♖xg7? ♖g8 19 ♖xg8 ♖xg8 20 g3 h5 is a lot more trouble than it's worth) 18...g6 19 bxc4 ♗xc4 (19...♘xc4 would also be met by 20 ♘xc4 and d3, with a similar advantage to the game) 20 ♘xc4 ♘xc4 21 d3 ♘b6 22 a4! *(D)*.

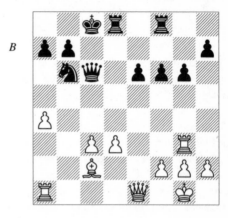

Playing on the queenside – the knight will be kicked, and White can generate an attack on the black king. 22...e5 23 a5 ♘d5 24 d4 ♕c7 (taking on d4 and opening the c-file is not very advisable, since the black king and queen make very tempting targets) 25 a6 b6 26 c4 ♕xc4 27 dxe5 ♘f4 28 ♖e3 ♔b8 29 e6 ♕c6 30 ♗e4 ♕xe6 31 ♗f3 ♕d7 32 ♖e7 ♖fe8 33 ♕e4! (this is an excellent attacking concept – it's a shame that time-trouble prevented its completion) 33...♘e2+ 34 ♔f1 ♕xe7 35 ♕a8+ ♔c7 36 ♕c6+ ♔b8 37 ♕a8+ ♔c7 38 ♕b7+ ♔d6 39 ♖d1+?? (39 ♕c6+ ♔e5 40 ♕e4+ ♔d6 41 ♖d1+ ♔c5 42 ♕c2+ ♔b5 43 ♗c6+ ♔b4 44 ♖b1+ ♔a5 45 ♕a4# was the way to do it) 39...♔e6 40 ♖e1 ♔f7 0-1 Pavasović-Wells, European Ch, Warsaw 2005.

8 ♕e2 *(D)*

No prizes for this one – the e5-pawn was attacked and this is the only way to defend it.

8...g5!

I can understand the difficulty an inexperienced player might have in understanding this move. After all, in most opening primers, there

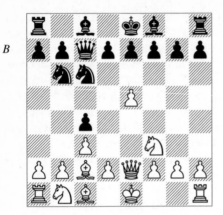

is an implicit rule that moving your g-pawn two squares forward is rarely a good idea. Here, however, it's positionally essential. Consider the following points:

- If both sides simply develop, then White will castle, bring a rook to e1, and play his knight to a3. Black will then suffer from a weak c4-pawn, a chronic lack of central space, and a purposeless development (the two knights and queen aren't doing very much if their attack on e5 isn't effective). So there is a real urgency required in Black's actions.
- The traditional arguments against playing ...g5 (and the reason why it should be avoided in most positions) are predicated on development (pawn moves don't develop pieces) and king safety. Looking at each in turn:

Development: Black is as developed as White. Furthermore, it will take several moves before White can complete development. Also, given that ...g5 gains time (White must deal with the threat of ...g4, winning the e5-pawn) while preparing ...♗g7, in many ways it is a developing move.

King Safety: The black king has not committed itself to the kingside yet (though it can often end up there, as occurs in this game). Furthermore, the position is quite closed, meaning that the potential tactical drawbacks of such an audacious move as ...g5 are limited.

- The move makes a lot of structural sense. Black is trying to exchange a g-pawn for an e-pawn, and in most cases a central pawn is worth more than one on the side.

In practice, Black has played 8...g5 with near-universal regularity, though 8...e6 hasn't been refuted. After the logical 9 b3 g5 10 ♘a3 g4 11 ♘b5 ♕b8 12 ♘g5 ♘xe5 13 bxc4, as played in Kuijf-Stripunsky, Wijk aan Zee 1996, a complex position arises after either capture on c4, though I like White's chances since Black will need a lot of skill to hold his whole position together – in particular, his dark squares seem very weak.

9 h3

Obviously 9 ♘xg5? ♕xe5 gives Black a beautiful endgame.

White has one major alternative though: 9 e6, aiming to disrupt the black structure before taking on g5. Tiviakov gives this move a good write-up: "[9 e6] almost forcibly leads to an endgame that is very complex and difficult to understand too. If Black doesn't exchange queens, he can lose very quickly, as in the game Tiviakov-Czarnota. This sharp endgame occurred in my games against Van Wely and Ranola. Black can probably reach an equal position. But even then he has a hard life if he doesn't know what to do." 9...dxe6 10 ♘xg5 (D) and now:

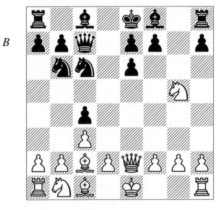

a) 10...h6 11 ♘e4 ♗d7 (Tiviakov suggests ...♘e5, either here or on the next move) 12 ♘a3 0-0-0 13 b3 ♘e5 14 bxc4 ♘exc4 15 d4 ♖g8 16 ♘xc4 ♘xc4 17 0-0 ♗c6 18 ♗d3 ♗d5 19 ♖b1 f5 20 ♘g3 ♔d7?? (but Black was already in deep trouble) 21 ♖b5 ♘d6 22 ♖c5 1-0 Tiviakov-Czarnota, European Ch, Warsaw 2005.

b) 10...♕e5 11 d4 cxd3 12 ♗xd3 ♕xe2+ 13 ♗xe2 h6 14 ♘e4 e5 15 ♘g3 e6! (this was an interesting novelty from Van Wely – previously, Black had played 15...♗e6) 16 0-0 f5 17 ♖d1 ♗d7 18 ♘h5 ♗e7 19 ♘d2 ♖d8 20 ♘c4 ♘xc4 21 ♗xc4 ♔f7 and Black had equalized in Tiviakov-Van Wely, Enschede 2005, though he went on to lose.

9...♗g7

Further increasing the pressure against the e5-pawn.

10 0-0

White plays this in order to reduce Black's options for taking on e5 – the queen is now out of the question, while the bishop wouldn't be advisable either.

10...♘xe5 11 ♘xg5 d5! *(D)*

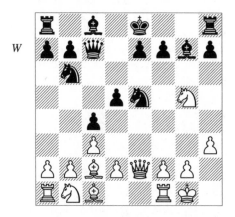

Black has an extra central pawn, and starts asserting his control with this aggressive and excellent move.

Why would White play such a position? There are three reasons:

1) The black kingside is loose following the disappearance of his g-pawn. He needs further preparation in order to castle at all, and once he does, his king isn't guaranteed safety.

2) The black centre could prove vulnerable. When Black's c4-pawn is exchanged for White's d-pawn, the d5-pawn will be open to attack.

3) The b6-knight is vulnerable to a rapid advance of the white a-pawn.

12 a4

This position has resulted in a relatively modest haul for Tiviakov – he scored just 1½/4 against Radjabov, Shabalov, Gladyszev and Sakaev.

12...♘g6

This is at least rare, if not a new move.

12...♗d7 is the most obvious attempt – Black develops his last piece and gives himself the option of queenside castling if necessary. While some games have proceeded with 13 ♖e1, I think White should immediately push the black knight to a dodgy square with 13 a5 ♘c8, and now he has a choice:

a) Black responded accurately to 14 d4 in Tiviakov-Shabalov, Isle of Man 2005: 14...cxd3 15 ♗xd3 ♘d6 16 ♖e1 0-0-0 17 ♘f3 ♘c6 18 a6 b6 19 ♘a3 e5 and Black went on to win.

b) 14 ♘f3 ♘g6 15 d4 cxd3 *(D)* and then:

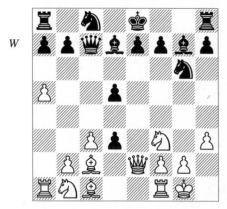

b1) 16 ♕xd3 e6 17 ♖e1 ♘ce7 18 a6 e5 19 axb7 ♕xb7 20 ♕a6 ♕c7 21 ♕a5 ♕b7 ½-½ Tiviakov-Radjabov, Warsaw 2005. The main line of Tiviakov's analysis runs 22 c4 dxc4 23 ♘xe5 ♘xe5 24 ♖xe5 ♗xe5 25 ♕xe5 ♖g8 26 ♗e4 ♗c6 27 ♘c3 f5 28 ♘b5 ♖g6 29 ♕h8+ ♔d7 30 ♕d4+ ♔e8 31 ♕h8+ with a draw by perpetual check.

b2) 16 ♗xd3 e5 17 a6 ♘ce7 (17...b6 18 c4 dxc4 19 ♗e4 ♖b8 20 ♘c3 ♘ce7 21 ♘d5 ♘xd5 22 ♗xd5 ♗c6 23 ♕xc4 was better for White in Tiviakov-Gladyszev, Isle of Man 2005) 18 axb7 ♕xb7 19 ♗a6 ♕c7 20 ♘a3 0-0 21 ♘b5 ♕c6 22 ♗e3 ♘f5 23 ♖fd1 ♘xe3 24 fxe3 ♕b6 with an edge for Black, Tiviakov-Sakaev, Khanty-Mansiisk (World Cup) 2005.

13 d4

White refrains from 13 a5 since the b6-knight wants to move anyway – here it has a good square on d7 rather than a passive one on c8.

13...cxd3

If Black doesn't play this, his g7-bishop will be restricted and he'll be left with less central space.

14 ♗xd3 ♘d7

This move can be viewed as a concession of sorts, since White has saved time by not playing a5. However, Black doesn't have any useful waiting moves. 14...0-0 just loses to 15 ♕h5, and kicking the knight is inadvisable: 14...h6 15 ♘f3 0-0 16 ♘a3 a6 17 a5 and the knight is forced to a4, since 17...♘d7 18 ♗xg6 fxg6 19 ♕e6+ is very strong.

15 ♖e1 ♕d6 16 ♘a3 a6 17 ♘f3 (D)

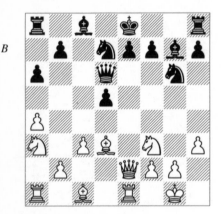

An interesting retreat – Pavasović is happy to let Epishin castle, as long as pressure can be exerted on the black centre.

17...0-0 18 ♗e3

18 ♗xg6 fxg6 19 ♕xe7 ♕xe7 20 ♖xe7 ♘c5! is fine for Black – there's no convenient way to defend the a4-pawn.

18...e5

Epishin plays thematically, but his centre is about to come under enormous pressure.

19 ♖ad1 ♕c6?

As silly as it looks, 19...f5!! was the only way to play the position, radically stopping ♗f5. After 20 ♗c4 ♘f6 21 ♗g5 e4 22 ♘h4 ♘e5 Black is completely fine since 23 ♗xf6? ♕xf6 24 ♗xd5+ ♔h8 25 g3 ♘d3 leaves White with big problems.

20 ♗f5!

Both avoiding the threatened ...e4 and hitting a major defender of the black centre.

20...e4

It takes some experience to realize just how undesirable this advance is for Black. Beginners (and, perhaps, some club players) will rejoice in 'gaining space', 'gaining time', 'preparing a kingside attack' and all the other things which this move could be misconstrued as doing. In fact, his centre has just lost all its flexibility, which means that it's easier to attack. When playing against black pawns on d5 and e5, White has to look out for both the ...d4 and ...e4 advances all the time, and has access to few central squares; in the present structure, the black pawns have no conceivable advances, plus White now has the d4-outpost for a knight.

20...♘c5 tries to keep the pawns abreast of each other, but 21 ♗xg6 fxg6 22 ♘xe5! is a killing tactic. After 22...♗xe5 23 ♗xc5 ♕xc5 (23...♖e8 24 ♗e3 is also grim for Black) 24 ♕xe5 ♕xf2+ 25 ♔h2 White is dominant.

21 ♘d4 (D)

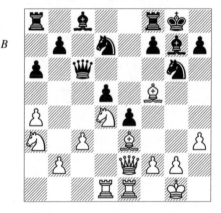

21...♕f6?

The queen is just vulnerable here. Black might as well have something to suffer for: 21...♕xa4 22 f3 exf3 23 ♕xf3 ♘de5 24 ♕f2!? and White has excellent compensation due to his kingside pressure, though Black is still very much in the game.

22 f3!

Dismantling the d5-e4 chain – where there used to be control, only weakness remains.

22...exf3

Trying to hold the e-pawn is no cakewalk either: 22...♘c5 23 fxe4 ♘xe4 24 ♗xe4 dxe4 25

♖f1 ♕e5 26 ♘c4 ♕g3 27 ♗f2 ♕c7 28 a5 and White is dominant – Black has major weaknesses on b6 and e4, and he'll probably end up getting crushed.

23 ♕xf3

This is a critical position for Black.

23...♘h4?!

Poorly judged, and probably the result of frustration. 23...♘de5 is more tenacious, though after something like 24 ♕h5 ♖e8 25 ♘ac2! (improving the worst-placed piece) 25...♕d8 26 ♘b4 ♗e6 27 ♗h6 the white position just plays itself.

24 ♕h5 ♘g6

A forced retreat. 24...♘xf5 25 ♘xf5 is simply crushing, since Black's position can't withstand the exchange of his dark-squared bishop, especially when its counterpart remains on e3. For instance, 25...♘e5 26 ♘xg7 ♕xg7 27 ♗h6 and Black loses the house.

25 ♘ac2! (D)

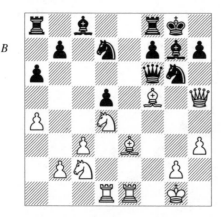

Dragging the a3-knight into the game.

25...♕d6

Epishin frees the f6-square for his knight, so that it can defend the kingside.

26 ♗h6! ♘f6 27 ♕g5

Black has temporarily managed to cover his king, but the g7-bishop can't avoid an exchange.

27...♘e4

Desperately trying to complicate, but it's not enough (or it shouldn't be, at least).

Black could have forced an exchange of queens with 27...♗xh6 28 ♕xh6 ♕f4, but his troubles persist in the endgame: 29 ♕xf4 ♘xf4

30 ♗xc8 ♖axc8 31 ♖f1 ♘6h5 32 ♔h2 ♘e6 33 ♘f5 and Black drops a pawn for starters.

28 ♗xe4 ♗xh6

This was the idea. Naturally, 28...dxe4 isn't too bright after 29 ♗xg7, when Black can't take in view of 30 ♘f5+.

29 ♕xh6 dxe4 30 ♖xe4 f5 (D)

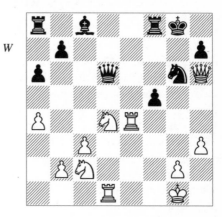

Retreating the rook now gives White an easily winning position. However, at this point the game score becomes incomprehensible. The players apparently stopped recording a few moves later, and the game somehow ended in a draw. The game has been instructive enough up to this point, so the rest of the game doesn't matter for our purposes.

Conclusions

1) 6...c4 is the most ambitious move for Black and, in my opinion, is also the best. It exploits the main problem with delaying d4 – the fact that Black can take *en passant* means that the e5-pawn is seriously weakened.

2) In the battle between 7...♕c7 and 7...d6, my money is on 7...♕c7. 7...d6 leads to difficult middlegames for Black in which he struggles to gain enough central control – certainly, the two Pavasović games in the notes constitute a serious deterrent to anyone intending to adopt this line.

3) 9 e6 leads to a roughly level endgame. There is still plenty of play in the position, but I don't think White can claim an advantage.

4) In the main line after 9 h3, an extremely unbalanced middlegame is reached. Black has full central occupation, but White can try to

chip away at the e5- and d5-pawns. I think 12...♗d7 is looking like the most reliable move at the moment, but this can only be an interim evaluation.

5) My overall conclusion is that, after 6...c4, Black has a perfectly acceptable opening position. I think this move constitutes the main argument against delaying d4.

Game 12
Sergei Tiviakov – Mircea Parligras
Solsona 2006

1 e4 c5 2 c3 ♘f6 3 e5 ♘d5 4 ♗c4

The latest fashion. Tiviakov has been flirting with the move, though he still retains a strong preference for 4 ♘f3 (I think 4 d4 has almost vanished from his repertoire). The threat to the knight can be combined with a quick opening of the d-file to create active play for White. Of course, there are numerous direct transpositions into other lines, most notably with 4...♘b6 5 ♗b3 c4 6 ♗c2 ♘c6 7 ♘f3 ♕c7.

4...e6 *(D)*

Black only has two decent moves here, and this is one of them. 4...♕c7 is premature in view of 5 ♘f3! (not 5 ♗xd5?? ♕xe5+).

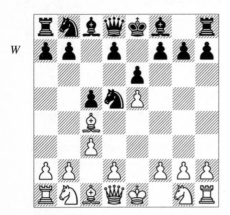

5 d4

Subtly, this move begins the process of opening the d-file since White has the option of dxc5 (or meeting ...cxd4 with ♕xd4).

5 ♘f3 is of course an alternative. Then:

a) 5...d6 6 exd6 ♗xd6 7 d4 cxd4 8 ♕xd4 0-0 9 0-0 ♘c6 10 ♕e4 ♘de7 11 ♘g5 ♘g6 12 h4 gave White some initiative in Tiviakov-Castano, Neiva 2005.

b) 5...♘b6 is a move that I suppose is prompted by a fear of ♗xd5 at some point, but this move comes with light-square costs for White in addition to structural ones for Black. We shall follow the game Ponomariov-Van Wely, Khanty-Mansiisk (World Cup) 2005, which became a rout: 6 ♗b3 d6 7 exd6 ♗xd6 (if Van Wely was planning to take on d4, it would have made sense to have the queen make this capture, and put the bishop on e7) 8 0-0 ♘c6 9 d4 cxd4 (after 9...0-0 10 dxc5 ♗xc5 11 ♘bd2 and 12 ♘e4, White has some initiative) 10 cxd4 ♘d5 (10...0-0 is much safer, though I still like White in view of the badly-placed black pieces on b6 and d6) 11 ♗g5! *(D)*.

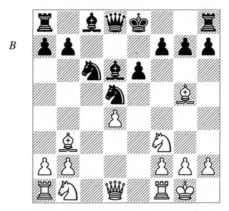

This poses unpleasant problems for Black. 11...♗e7 (11...♕a5 is an alternative, and after 12 ♗d2 ♕d8 White can repeat or get a pleasant edge with 13 ♗xd5 exd5 14 ♖e1+ ♗e6 15 ♘g5) 12 ♗xd5 ♕xd5 (12...♗xg5 is inaccurate, since 13 ♗xc6+ bxc6 14 ♘xg5 ♕xg5 leaves Black with a very poor bishop on c8, restricted by the pawns on c6 and e6; after 15 ♘d2!

followed by ♘b3 and ♖c1, Black can only beg for a draw) 13 ♘c3 ♕f5 (13...♕d6 is the alternative, when 14 ♗xe7 ♘xe7 15 ♘e5! gives White a nice IQP position because his pieces are so active) 14 ♗xe7 ♘xe7 15 ♕a4+ (15 ♖e1 0-0 16 ♘e5 is a good alternative, but Ponomariov wants to keep the black king in the centre) 15...♗d7 (15...♘c6 is hopeless in view of the thematic 16 d5! exd5 17 ♖ae1+ ♗e6 18 ♘d4 ♕f4 19 ♘xe6 ♕xa4 20 ♘c5+ ♕e4 21 ♘3xe4 dxe4 22 ♖xe4+, when White's activity constitutes a decisive advantage) 16 ♕a3 (the black king is now stuck in the centre) 16...♘d5 (16...♘c6 17 ♘e5 is also very pleasant for White) 17 ♘e5 ♘xc3?! (opening the b-file spells the beginning of the end) 18 bxc3 ♕g5 19 ♖ab1 ♗c8 20 ♖fe1 ♕e7 21 ♕a4+ ♔f8 (now Black will never be able to castle, and Ponomariov has a choice of wins) 22 d5! (extremely strong, and thematic for both IQP-type positions and ones where the opposing king is stuck in the middle) 22...h5 23 ♖bd1 exd5 (Black gives up his queen in order to prevent the further march of the d-pawn, but with his pieces on such terrible squares it's not really surprising that he can't cobble a defence together) 24 ♘g6+ fxg6 25 ♖xe7 ♔xe7 26 ♕d4 ♔f7 27 ♕xd5+ ♔f6 28 ♕d4+ ♔f7 29 ♕c4+ ♗e6 30 ♖d7+ 1-0. A crisp attacking effort by Ponomariov.

We return to 5 d4 (D):

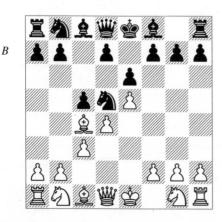

Black now chose to sacrifice a pawn:
5...cxd4
This opens the d-file.

5...d6 is the alternative: after 6 exd6 cxd4 7 ♗xd5 exd5 8 ♕xd4 ♕xd6 (8...♘c6 9 ♕xd5 transposes to the note to Black's 5th move) Black hangs on to his material, at the cost of an IQP. Now 9 ♘e2!? was Tiviakov's novelty, usefully covering the e-file and preparing to play ♗f4. 9...♘c6 10 ♕d3 ♗e6 (Tiviakov suggests 10...♗e7 11 0-0 0-0, intending ...♘e5; the immediate 10...♘e5 runs into 11 ♕g3) 11 ♗f4 ♕d7 12 ♘d2 ♗e7 13 ♘b3 0-0 14 0-0 ♖fe8 15 ♘ed4 ♘xd4 16 ♘xd4 ♗c5 17 ♖fe1 ♗g4 18 ♗e3 ♗f8 19 h3 ♗h5 20 ♕b5 ♖ad8 21 ♕xd7 ♖xd7 with an unpleasant endgame for Black, Tiviakov-Neverov, European Ch, Warsaw 2005. All of his attacking chances have evaporated, and he's left with a grim defence of the IQP. White won after a long grind.

6 ♗xd5
Naturally, White isn't compelled to do this, but it does represent an interesting alternative to the main lines. 6 cxd4 d6 would transpose to a main variation, but one where White's bishop is well placed on c4. I'm not sure how Black could exploit the position of this bishop with a different continuation.

6...exd5 7 ♕xd4! (D)
Clearly the critical test. It's hard to believe that Black can have real problems after 7 cxd4, since he just plays ...d6 at a suitable moment.

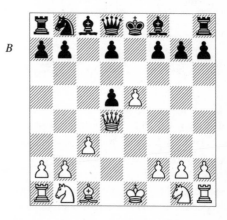

7...♘c6
There's no way to defend the d5-pawn, so Black brings a knight into play and begins to liquidate the centre, which should favour the better-developed side.

8 ♕xd5 d6!

In such a new position, all conclusions are provisional, but this certainly seems like the best move.

9 exd6

Even though this helps develop Black's kingside, it has to be played. The endgame after 9 ♘f3?! dxe5 10 ♕xd8+ ♔xd8 holds no dangers for Black – in fact, I even prefer his position due to his central control and extra centre pawn.

9...♗xd6

This is the most natural move, preparing to castle.

It's rare that a pawn such as the one on d6 can be tolerated for long, and if Black tries to work around it he runs into problems. For instance, 9...♗e6 can be met by 10 d7+! ♗xd7 11 ♘f3 ♗e7 12 0-0 0-0, when both 13 ♗e3 and 13 ♗g5 leave Black struggling to demonstrate enough compensation.

10 ♗g5 (D)

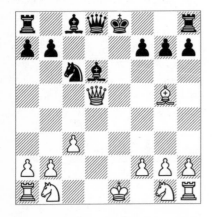

This is a new move by Tiviakov. It's interesting that Fritz, which is normally a rather materialistic beast, thinks the chances are equal here, even though Black is a pawn down and has only one more minor piece developed than White does. The machine must be taking two factors into account: first, Black's two bishops represent a long-term asset (let's say they're worth about half a pawn); second, the white knights will have trouble finding active squares (the c3-pawn takes a natural spot away from the queen's knight, while the king's knight will probably end up on e2 to plug the e-file).

10...♘e7

I'm never a huge fan of repeatedly moving developed pieces instead of bringing fresh forces into the game, and this doubly applies when material down. 10...♕c7! is a good alternative. The line-up on the b8-h2 diagonal gives Black some threats against the h2-pawn. A possible continuation might run 11 ♕e4+ ♗e6 12 ♘f3 0-0 13 0-0 ♖fe8 and, in my opinion, Black has full compensation.

11 ♕f3

The queen takes a natural square away from the knight, but Black's active possibilities have also been reduced, since the e7-knight is pinned to the queen and will take a couple of moves to get to a juicy square.

11...0-0 12 ♘e2 ♕b6

Unpinning the knight and creating a threat against the b2-pawn.

13 b3 (D)

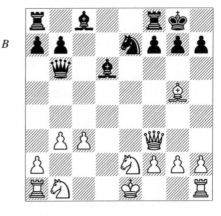

This constitutes a very slight weakening of the queenside structure – so slight, in fact, that I don't think Black can exploit it, though he can certainly try harder than he does in the game.

13...♕b5?

I think this is misjudged. 13...♘g6 retains the knight and given rise to more active possibilities:

a) After 14 0-0, 14...♕b5! is now much more effective; e.g., 15 ♗d2 ♘e5 (the knight is harassing the white queen, and will create an attack on the h2-pawn) 16 ♕e4 ♘g4 (there's no easy way to meet the threat) 17 ♘g3 ♗xg3 18 fxg3 ♘xh2!.

b) 14 ♘d2 ♘e5 15 ♕e4 ♘g4 16 ♗h4 ♗e6 and Black has masses of play.

14 ♗xe7!

Two bishops, without complementary advantages in activity, structure or development, can't compensate for a pawn. Had Tiviakov retreated instead, Black would have gained time for his attack (transposing into the note to his 13th move).

14...♗xe7 *(D)*

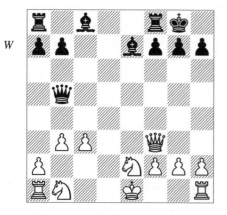

15 ♘d2

Black is now struggling to show any real initiative.

15...a5?

This doesn't help much. Black wants to bring his rook into play via a6, as in many lines of the Budapest Defence, but here this plan seems too slow.

16 0-0 ♖a6 17 ♘d4 ♕d7 18 ♖ad1 ♖g6 19 ♖fe1 b6 20 ♘c4 ♖f6 21 ♘e5 *(D)*

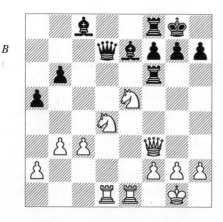

The bishops don't look like outperforming the knights any time soon. One odd consequence of Black's pawn-loss is that he no longer has the necessary central pawns to cover his centre squares.

21...♕c7 22 ♕g3!

Setting up some very nasty threats against the whole black monarchy.

22...♗c5??

This is the losing blunder, but Black was already in time-trouble, and he had no compensation for the pawn anyway.

23 ♘g4! *(D)*

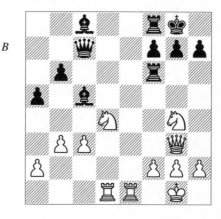

Simultaneously threatening the black queen and rook.

23...♖f4 24 ♘f6+! 1-0

24...♔h8 25 ♘e8! is a beautiful finish.

Conclusions

1) Coming up with a new opening line on move 4 is quite an achievement, and Tiviakov has been suitably rewarded so far. There is little doubt that 4 ♗c4 poses novel problems for Black.

2) Black has a major choice on move 4. Dropping the knight back to b6 and transposing to Game 11, Pavasović-Epishin, would be my choice, but there's nothing wrong with 4...e6.

3) After 5 d4, Black has a choice between a passive position with equal material, and a pawn sacrifice. I recommend that he sheds the pawn, though it must be followed up precisely. After Tiviakov's 10 ♗g5, 10...♕c7! provides good play for the sacrificed material.

4 2...d5: Black Plays ...♘f6 and ...e6

1 e4 c5 2 c3 d5

Having dealt with one of the two main defences, 2...♘f6, in some detail, we now turn to the other one. Black gains space in the centre and hits the e4-pawn, safe in the knowledge that his queen will be able to recapture on d5 without losing time since ♘c3 is impossible.

3 exd5

No other move deserves serious attention, since if Black can develop his light-squared bishop and play ...e6 while maintaining a pawn in the middle, there will be no reason to prefer White's position.

3...♕xd5 4 d4 ♘f6

Black develops his king's knight to its natural square, and conveniently defends his queen at the same time.

5 ♘f3

White can try other moves, but this seems to be best. Now he's just a couple of moves away from castling. His next move will be determined by Black's approach. In this chapter, we examine one of the main defences, based around an early ...e6.

5...e6

Just preparing to develop the bishop and castle. It is far from straightforward for White to demonstrate an advantage against this line. We shall focus on the following:

6 ♗e3. I've always believed this to be the most dangerous line, but Game 13, S.B.Hansen-Krasenkow, shows a relatively new approach for Black which has been achieving excellent results.

6 ♘a3 is a very logical move, since ♘b5 is a major threat. Game 14, Tiviakov-Van Wely, shows some of the ideas.

6 ♗e2 and others don't seem too threatening, but contain some poison: have a look at Game 15, Rublevsky-Vitiugov, for a model demonstration of what White is aiming for.

Game 13
Sune Berg Hansen – Michal Krasenkow
Bundesliga 2004/5

Michal Krasenkow is a serious theoretician. He knows his lines inside out and frequently contributes novelties in his favourite systems. Hence, anything he plays is worth noticing.

1 e4 c5 2 ♘f3 e6 3 c3 d5 4 exd5 ♕xd5 5 d4 ♘f6 6 ♗e3 (D)

This is an attempt to force Black to capture on d4, since now dxc5 is threatened.

6...cxd4

Agreeing to the IQP position.

6...♘bd7 is the alternative. Now dxc5 is useless since Black can recapture the pawn after an exchange of queens on d1. After 7 c4 ♕d6 8 ♘c3 cxd4 9 ♘xd4 a6! (it's important to prevent ♘db5) 10 ♗e2 ♕c7 11 0-0 b6 12 ♗f3 White was a little better in Erenburg-Kacheishvili, European Ch, Istanbul 2003, since his pieces are more active and he has a lead in development.

7 cxd4

It's obvious that White's next move will be ♘c3, developing the knight to its best square and hitting the black queen. Therefore, this isn't the time to play by rote or make a quick move –

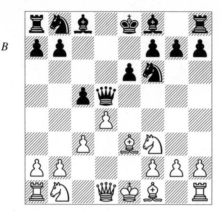

what Black chooses right now will affect the entire middlegame.

7...♗b4+

This annoying move is scoring heavily in practice. White can't get his normal IQP positions, and must instead struggle in a tricky positional game.

7...♘c6 8 ♘c3 ♕d6 9 a3 ♗e7 10 ♗d3 0-0 is a typical IQP position. White can play 11 0-0, which leaves him with some pretty promising play, but 11 ♕c2!? poses original problems. This line has been extensively used, with great success, by GM Joel Benjamin. The point is that Black can't play the natural 11...b6? because he loses a pawn after 12 ♘e4 ♘xe4 13 ♗xe4 with a fork on c6 and h7. Instead, Black should try 11...♗d7 12 0-0 ♖ac8 13 ♖ad1 ♖fd8 14 ♖fe1 ♗e8 with a balanced game. If Black is worried about this line, he can play 10...b6, followed by fianchettoing his bishop and castling.

8 ♘c3 (D)

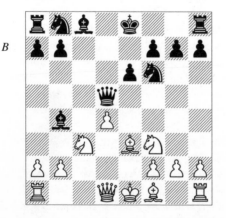

8...0-0

This is natural and very probably best.

Cheekier players might be tempted to play 8...♕a5, but I think White can easily deal with this diversion: 9 ♕b3 0-0 10 ♗c4 with strong development.

8...♗d7 9 ♗d3 ♗b5 10 0-0 ♗xc3 11 bxc3 0-0 is the principal alternative, with a position that can also be reached via the move-order 8...0-0 9 ♗d3 ♗d7 10 0-0 ♗xc3 11 bxc3 ♗b5 (my thanks to IM Mark Quinn for drawing my attention to this move). After 12 ♗xb5 ♕xb5 13 ♖b1 ♕a6 14 ♕b3 b6 we have similar play to the game, though it is the black queen, rather than the knight, which needs to rejoin play from a6. Vajda-Balogh, Tusnad 2005 continued 15 ♗g5 ♘bd7 16 c4 ♖ac8 17 ♘d2 ♕a5 18 ♕g3 with a pleasant game for White.

9 ♗d3

This is such a natural move that I'm sure many players wouldn't think much about alternatives, but White's other options might be more promising – they're definitely more complex:

a) 9 a3 isn't as stupid as it looks, since after 9...♗xc3+ 10 bxc3 b6 White can retain his light-squared bishop with 11 c4. This keeps a little more tension than the game continuation.

b) 9 ♗e2 b6 10 ♘e5 is a critical alternative, aiming to play ♗f3. After 10...♘e4 (10...♗a6 11 ♗f3 ♘e4 12 ♕a4! is good for White) 11 ♕c2 ♗a6 12 ♗f3 f5, 13 ♘d3 ♘c6 14 0-0 ♗xc3 15 bxc3 ♗xd3 16 ♕xd3 ♘e5 17 ♗xe4 ♘xd3 18 ♗xd5 exd5 gave Black a nice endgame in Shaw-Kurajica, Calvia Olympiad 2004, but 13 ♕a4! would have posed some problems.

9...b6 (D)

Giving the bishop two attractive development options.

10 0-0

Now the pin has been broken and the black queen is under attack.

10...♗xc3

10...♕d8 leaves the bishop misplaced on b4 – it would rather be on e7. If he wants to take on c3 he should do so immediately.

11 bxc3 ♗a6!?

This is the point, and has been known for a long time – GM Alexander Kotov (famous in

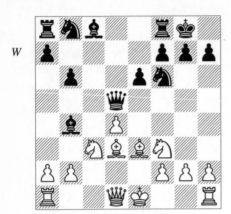

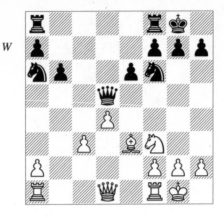

the chess world both for his superb book *Think Like a Grandmaster* and as a world-championship candidate) played in this fashion back in 1942, but the line was then abandoned for over 50 years.

White can't hold on to his two bishops, and instead must play a simplified position with hanging pawns. I've misassessed this position for quite a while. At first, I preferred Black, which is just wrong. Then I wrote that "the position is equal at the moment but I would prefer the black pieces, since he has most of the long-term chances." This is also unjustified. I now agree with Rozentalis and Harley when they write that "[This line] has scored very well for Black, but White should have a comfortable game as he can establish a pawn-centre that is not vulnerable and gives him a lot of space". I had assumed that, with two pairs of minor pieces exchanged, Black's lack of space wouldn't be a big deal, but in fact the space advantage is still quite significant, not least because White has all of the active play, on both sides of the board.

11...♗b7 12 c4 ♕d6 looks a little better for White – he retains the two bishops and has seized some space in the middle. Fritz wants to create a passed pawn immediately by playing 13 c5, but I don't think this is necessary – just put the queen on e2 and bring the rooks to c1 and d1.

12 ♗xa6

It's definitely worth dragging the black knight to this inferior square.

12...♘xa6 *(D)*

13 ♕e2

I don't think this has the required urgency – White has to create some play quite soon in order to avoid falling into an inferior position.

a) 13 ♕d3 ♘c5! is a nice trick which leaves Black with a comfortable position – to be honest, I don't know if this knight is heading for e4 or d7, but it looks fine for Black in either case.

b) 13 ♕a4 ♕b7 (13...♘b8 isn't popular for some reason, maybe because of 14 c4 ♕e4 15 ♘e5, when the b8-knight has some problems developing) 14 c4 is the main line, with a more active position than White achieves in our main game. Collins-Volpinari, Turin Olympiad 2006 is quite instructive: 14...♖fc8 15 ♖fc1 ♘b8 16 ♕b5 ♘bd7 17 a4 ♕c6 18 ♕b3 ♖ab8 19 ♗f4 ♖a8 (19...♖b7 is very strongly met by 20 d5!) 20 h3 h6 21 a5 ♘e4 22 ♕e3 ♘ef6 (this back-and-forth manoeuvring looks pointless, but in fact it's hard to suggest any active possibilities for Black – for instance, if he plays 22...♘d6, then 23 d5! is very strong, while the text-move loses control of the e5-square) 23 ♕b3 ♘e4 24 ♕b2 ♘ef6 25 ♖a3!! (the rook-lift is a well-known concept in hanging-pawn positions; the nice thing about this move is its flexibility – White can play on the a-file {with ♕a2}, the b-file {with axb6 and ♖b3} or the kingside, as occurs in the game) 25...♘e4 26 ♕e2 ♘ef6 27 ♘e5 ♘xe5 28 ♗xe5 *(D)*.

This position is extremely unpleasant for Black. His plan of bringing the queen to the kingside doesn't work out so well, but 28...♘d7 29 ♖g3 leaves White far more active. Incidentally, while 28...♘d5 is possible since the

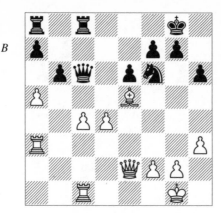

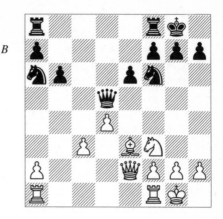

c-pawn is pinned, it doesn't change much: 29 ♖g3 with an attack.

The game continued: 28...♕e4 29 ♖e3 ♕g6 30 ♖g3 ♕f5 31 ♖e1 (I couldn't play the immediate 31 ♖f3 in view of 31...♕e4; however, 31 ♕e3 or 31 ♕d2 would have won material in view of the dual threats of ♕xh6 and ♖f3 followed by ♗xf6) 31...♞e8 32 a6! (much stronger than taking on b6 – now the a7-pawn is fixed as a weakness and Black doesn't get any counterplay on the c-file) 32...♖c6 33 ♖f3 ♕g6 34 ♕a2!? (the immediate break in the centre was also possible, but I preferred to prepare it) 34...♖ac8 35 d5 exd5 (I had missed that after 35...♖xc4 36 d6 Black has 36...♖e4!; that said, it's still quite apparent that White has overwhelming compensation, as nicely illustrated by the following forced line: 37 ♖xe4 ♕xe4 38 ♖e3 ♕c6 39 ♖c3 ♕d7 40 ♖xc8 ♕xc8 41 ♕a4 ♞f6 42 ♗xf6 gxf6 43 g3 f5 44 d7 ♕c1+ 45 ♔g2 ♕c7 46 ♕d4 ♕d8 47 ♕d6 and the queen endgame is a trivial win for White, since ♕c6-b7xa7 is unstoppable) 36 cxd5 ♖c2 37 ♕a4 ♖2c4 38 ♕d7 f6 39 ♗f4 ♔h7 40 ♖g3 ♕h5 41 ♖xe8 1-0 Collins-Volpinari, Turin Olympiad 2006.

We now return to 13 ♕e2 (D):

13...♞b8!

This enables the black queen to be more actively placed than after 13...♕b7. Byway suggests 13...b5 14 a4 ♕c4, which is worth thinking about, but I prefer Krasenkow's move.

14 c4 ♕e4!

In contrast to the position after 13 ♕a4, here Black has both centralized his queen and rerouted his knight to a better square.

15 ♕b2 ♞bd7

We now have a typical 'hanging pawns' structure, as discussed at length in many texts on chess strategy.

16 a4

A typical minority attack, trying to create a weakness on b6. White has few prospects of a kingside attack, so it makes sense to play on the queenside.

16...♖ac8 17 ♖ac1 ♖c7 18 ♖fe1 ♖fc8 (D)

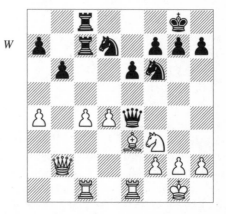

Black's pieces are perfectly placed, and he is the only one with any chances of an advantage.

19 ♕b3 ♕f5 20 h3 ♞e4 21 a5 h6

21...♕xa5 drops material to 22 ♗f4.

22 axb6 axb6

22...♞xb6?! is much riskier, since the white c-pawn becomes a major asset.

23 ♞h4 ♕f6 24 ♞f3 ♕f5 25 ♖e2

I'm not sure why White declined the repetition. Perhaps he just felt Krasenkow would avoid it (for instance, by 25 ♘h4 ♕a5!?) but I still think this would be a better version for White than he obtains in the game.

25...♖a8 26 ♖ec2 ♘ef6 27 ♗d2 ♖ca7!

Given the solid defence of the c-pawn, there was no point in pressurizing it further. Instead Krasenkow turns his attention to the a-file, in order to exchange a pair of rooks.

28 ♗b4

This seems to be shooting into thin air, but in fact he has a fiendish idea.

28...♖a1 29 ♕b2 ♕e4

A cute resource, since the c2-rook hangs after a mass exchange on a1. It doesn't change much though.

30 ♗e7!?

Trying to deflect the d7-knight.

30...♖xc1+ 31 ♖xc1 ♘h5 *(D)*

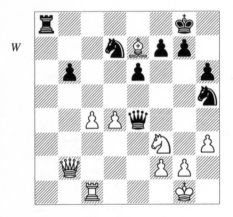

32 ♗d6

32 ♕b5 might be better. After a logical sequence like 32...♘f4 33 ♖e1 ♕b7 34 ♗d6 ♖a5 35 ♕b3 ♘g6 the game looks pretty balanced.

32...♕c6 33 ♗h2 ♘hf6 34 ♗e5 ♘e8 35 ♗f4 ♖a4 36 ♕b3 ♕a8 37 ♕b5 ♘ef6 38 ♗e5 ♖a5 39 ♕b1 ♘e4 40 ♗f4 ♖a2 41 ♕b5?

41 ♖e1 is better, since 41...♘xf2 is only good enough for perpetual after 42 ♗d2 ♘xh3+ 43 gxh3 ♕xf3 44 ♕xa2 ♕g3+.

41...♘xf2! *(D)*

I don't know if White missed this, or just misjudged the position after Black's 44th move.

42 ♖f1 ♘d3 43 ♗xh6 gxh6 44 ♕xd7 ♘f4!

Black has an extremely strong attack.

45 ♖f2 ♕a3 46 ♖xa2

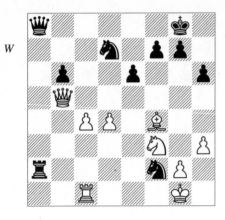

46 ♕d8+ ♔g7 47 ♕h4 drags the queen back into the defence and so avoids mate, but after 47...♕c1+ 48 ♔h2 ♘g6 49 ♕g3 ♖xf2 50 ♕xf2 ♕xc4 Black has an extra pawn, a safer king and excellent winning chances.

46...♕xa2 47 ♘h4 ♕xc4 48 ♕d8+ ♔g7 49 ♕xb6 ♕c1+ 50 ♔h2 ♕e1

Even in this simplified position, White has huge defensive problems, because queen and knight are a notoriously effective attacking pair. White is effectively playing a queen down.

51 ♕d8 ♘e2 52 ♘f3 ♕g3+ 53 ♔h1 ♘f4 54 ♘h4 ♘d3 55 ♘f3 ♘f2+ 56 ♔g1 ♘xh3+ 57 ♔h1 ♘f4 58 ♘h4 ♕g4 59 ♔h2 ♘d5 60 ♘f3 ♘e3 61 ♘h4 ♕f4+ 0-1

The finish could be 62 ♔h1 ♘g4 63 ♘f3 ♕c1+ 64 ♘g1 ♘f2+ 65 ♔h2 ♕f4+ 66 g3 ♘g4+ 67 ♔h3 ♕e4!, when White faces mate in at most six moves.

Conclusions

1) 6 ♗e3 poses Black some interesting problems. White tends to get advantages in space and activity at the cost of some structural weakening.

2) After the exchange on d4, Black has a choice between checking on b4 (and so keeping his queen on d5 for a while) and leaving White with an IQP. It's a simple matter of taste between these approaches, though (as far as I can tell) Black has been scoring much better with 7...♗b4+ than with 7...♘c6.

3) After 7...♘c6, I think an approach based on ♕c2 is an interesting way to handle the position. Black is denied his normal methods of

development, which means he needs either brains or preparation.

4) After 7...♗b4+, the main line leads to a position where White has a substantial space advantage but Black has some structural superiority and has exchanged a couple of pairs of minor pieces. White must play actively, as our main game graphically illustrates. However, with reasonably purposeful play White should keep a useful edge – moreover, I think these positions don't lend many winning chances to Black.

Game 14
Sergei Tiviakov – Loek van Wely
Wijk aan Zee 2006

1 e4 c5 2 c3 d5 3 exd5 ♕xd5 4 d4 e6 *(D)*

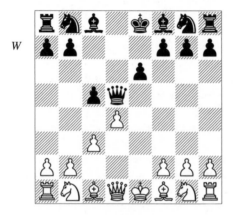

W

5 ♘f3

5 ♘a3 is a tricky sideline, playing for an early ♘b5. This can sometimes confuse one's opponent, though it's not a particularly exciting concept, not least because Black can avoid it with the move-order 4...♘f6 5 ♘f3 e6. In any case, it pays to know about such lines with both colours. Rozentalis and Harley give 5...♗d7 6 ♘b5 ♗xb5 7 ♗xb5+ ♘c6 as fine for Black – White has the two bishops, but that's the end of the good news about his position because 8...cxd4 is coming, hitting the b5-bishop. 8 ♕f3 cxd4 9 ♕xd5 exd5 10 cxd4 ♗b4+ 11 ♗d2 ♗xd2+ 12 ♔xd2 ♘ge7 leaves complete equality. In such a structure, a bishop is no better than a knight, so White can't even pretend that he has anything.

5...♘f6 6 ♘a3

This is White's latest attempt to generate something in the 4...e6 line. Jonathan Rowson gives a good account of the recent developments: "For the time being White has not come up with anything special in the lines with 6 ♗e3 where Black plays ...♗b4+ and tries to take on c3 followed by ...b6 and ...♗b7 *[I'd add that playing the bishop to a6 instead of b7 looks like a better equalizing attempt – S.C.].* 6 ♗d3 is not dangerous, unless Black takes on d4, which he doesn't need to, and 6 ♗e2 is generally thought to be fairly harmless. So that leaves us, for now, with 6 ♘a3."

6...♕d8! *(D)*

Taking the sting out of both ♗c4 and ♘b5.

6...♘c6 ignores the threat, and White does best to execute it immediately: 7 ♘b5! ♕d8 8 dxc5! (due to the weakness of the c7-square, Black can't play ...♕xd1+ but instead must allow his own king to be displaced) 8...♗xc5 9 ♕xd8+ ♔xd8 10 ♗f4 gives White more prospects of an advantage – moreover, Black's chances of winning such a position are virtually nil. It's quite clear why 6...♕d8 is the more popular option.

7 ♘c2

Initially, I was very sceptical of White's ability to generate anything real after this. His spatial and developmental advantages are minimal, and the position of his knight on c2 doesn't inspire confidence. A closer inspection of the position, however, reveals some factors in White's favour. His bishops have good squares (on d3 and g5), while the black pieces will struggle to establish meaningful activity. Also, ...cxd4 is a key resource for Black in such structures, but this would bring the c2-knight into the game. So I think it's fair to say that White has a normal

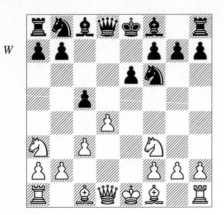

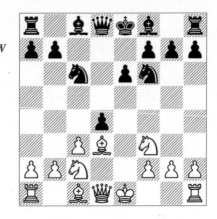

opening advantage here, though I believe Black can contain it with precise play.

7...♘c6

This is the most flexible – Black puts his knight on a natural square and keeps White guessing as to whether he'll opt for a defence based on ...♗e7 or ...cxd4 and ...♗c5.

8 ♗d3

Now Black has a decision to make.

8...cxd4

Opening things up and increasing the activity of both sides. Black also manages to exchange a pair of knights, which is in his favour since he has less space.

The solid 8...♗e7 9 0-0 0-0 is also playable, but Van Wely's move frees the c5-square for the bishop. White probably has an edge in either case. 10 ♕e2 poses some interesting problems. It seems that Black should take on d4 (thus solving the issue of the c2-knight for White), since 10...b6 is well met by 11 dxc5! bxc5 (Tiviakov gives 11...♗xc5 12 ♗g5 ♗b7 13 ♖ad1 ♕c7 14 ♗xf6 gxf6 15 ♕e4 f5 16 ♕h4 as clearly better for White) 12 ♗f4 ♕b6 13 ♘a3 ♘a5 14 ♘e5 ♗b7 15 ♗g5 ♖ad8 16 ♖ad1 ♗a8 17 ♖fe1 ♘c6 18 ♘ac4 ♕b7 19 ♘xc6 ♕xc6 20 f3 ♕c7 21 ♕e5!? ♕xe5 22 ♘xe5 and White had a very pleasant endgame in Tiviakov-Espig, Bad Wörishofen 2005.

We now return to 8...cxd4 (D):

9 ♘cxd4

It's extremely natural to improve the position of the c2-knight.

No prizes for other moves – avoiding exchanges with 9 cxd4?! leaves the knight badly

placed on c2 – its only good square is e3, but that would impede the dark-squared bishop.

9...♘xd4

Exchanging is clearly the strongest option, since otherwise Black's pawns would be compromised following ♘xc6, or else a piece would be passively placed in defending the knight.

10 ♘xd4

Again the most natural move, and again the best.

10 cxd4 is approximately equal, but I'd prefer to take Black since any further simplification would be to his benefit. I also dislike IQP positions when the opponent has ...♗b4+ which can't be met by ♘c3.

10...♗c5 (D)

This was a key idea of Black's 8th move, so it's the most consistent continuation. 10...♗e7 11 ♕f3 gives White more chances.

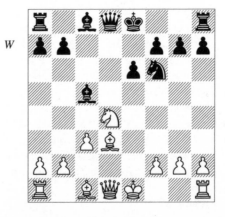

11 0-0

With this move, White transposes to a line of the Rubinstein French. The alternative is 11 ♗e3 ♗b6 (otherwise ♘xe6 would be embarrassing) 12 0-0 0-0 13 ♖e1. Now Beliavsky gives 13...♘d5 14 ♗d2 ♗xd4 15 cxd4 ♗d7 as equal – he has a few decades of top-level chess under his belt, so I think we should trust the assessment.

11...♗xd4!?

A risky decision, for obvious reasons – the dark squares immediately become more vulnerable.

11...0-0 is more standard: 12 ♗g5 h6 (putting the question to the bishop and preparing some *luft* for the king) 13 ♗h4 ♗xd4 (this exchange is by no means forced, but it seems like the cleanest way to equalize) 14 cxd4 ♗d7 15 ♖e1 ♗c6 16 ♖e5 ♖e8 17 ♕d2 ♔f8 18 ♗c4 g5!? (quite aggressive, but Black has enough central control to get away with it) 19 ♗g3 ♘e4 20 ♕e3 ♘d6 21 ♕a3 ♔g8 22 ♗d3 ♘f5 23 ♗xf5 exf5 24 ♖xe8+ ½-½ Godena-Bellini, Swiss Team Ch 2005 (this game was actually a Rubinstein French rather than a c3 Sicilian).

12 ♕a4+

Black has no comfortable way to deal with this check, since he wants to keep an eye on the d4-bishop.

12...♔e7!? *(D)*

Instead, 12...♗d7 13 ♕xd4 ♗c6 14 ♗e3 is very pleasant for White.

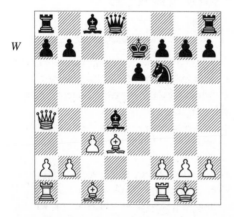

In structures of this type (more commonly arising from the French and the Caro-Kann), such king moves are a standard part of Black's

arsenal. Karpov alone has played dozens of games with ...♔e7 and ...♔f8. White will struggle to open the centre, so the king is reasonably secure, but the move is still as risky as it looks. One major factor, which generally isn't present in analogous French and Caro-Kann positions, is that Black has exchanged his dark-squared bishop for a knight. This leaves him exposed to some very unpleasant ideas on the a3-f8 diagonal if White can get a bishop there. I think the main question when Black makes such a move as ...♔e7 is this: can White generate some meaningful play before Black gets in ...♖e8, ...♔f8 and ...♔g8? Here, maybe he can.

13 cxd4

Tiviakov correctly avoids the exchange of queens in order to play against the black king.

Naturally 13 ♕xd4? ♕xd4 14 cxd4 is an endgame which only Black can win – one, moreover, where the king is ideally placed on e7.

13...♕d6 *(D)*

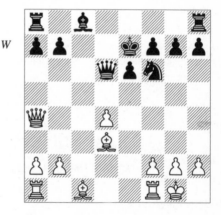

It's essential to gain control over some dark squares, and that's the point of this move. That said, the a3-f8 diagonal has just become twice as tempting for the dark-squared bishop.

14 b3

I think White missed a good chance here: 14 ♗d2 is a promising alternative, leaving the b3-square available to the queen. I think the black position is on shaky ground – for instance, 14...a5 can be met by the excellent 15 d5!!, when White has a clear advantage in all lines, viz. 15...♘xd5 16 ♗xa5 b6 17 ♕h4+ (one of the points of 15 d5) 17...♔f8 18 ♗d2 ♗a6 19 ♗xa6 ♖xa6 20 ♖fe1 and Black has continuing problems due to the incarceration of his rook on h8.

14...♗d7 15 ♕a5

15 ♗b5 is also interesting – it's not clear how the offensive capacity of the white bishop compares to the defensive capacity of the black one.

15...b6 *(D)*

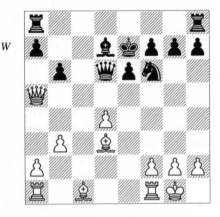

16 ♕e5

I imagine White was playing for a draw with this move. He could retain the queens with 16 ♕g5!? h6 17 ♕h4, which certainly seems like a more dynamic option.

16...♗c6 17 ♖d1

17 ♗g5 h6 18 ♗xf6+ gxf6 19 ♕e3 leaves the black king pretty secure – the cluster of pawns on e6, f6 and f7 do a good job of keeping the white pieces out.

17...h6 18 h3 ♖hd8 19 a4 ♕d5

19...♕xd4?? 20 ♗a3+ ♔e8 21 ♕c7 ♕d7 22 ♕g3 gives White a decisive attack.

20 ♗a3+ ♔e8 21 ♗f1 ♕xe5

The endgame is safe for Black.

22 dxe5 ♖xd1 23 ♖xd1 ♘d5 24 ♖d3 a6 25 ♖g3 ½-½

White has the two bishops, but Black has enough dark-square control to hold.

Conclusions

1) 6 ♘a3 is the kind of move one turns to after exhausting the alternatives. I don't think White has real chances of obtaining a serious advantage here. 6...♕d8 is almost essential, since otherwise 7 ♘b5 is too annoying.

2) In the main line, Black has an important decision to make at move 8. It seems like the c2-knight comes into play regardless of which line is selected. A solid approach with 8...♗e7 is quite possible, but I think that Van Wely's idea of transposing to a Rubinstein French is worth attention.

Game 15

Sergei Rublevsky – Nikita Vitiugov

Russian Ch semi-final, Kazan 2005

1 e4 c5 2 ♘f3 e6 3 c3

Sergei Rublevsky is well known for his narrow but very well-prepared opening repertoire. He has had some success with 3 c4 in the past, aiming for a Maroczy Bind structure, but now he seems to have transferred his allegiance to this version of the c3 Sicilian. The inclusion of ...e6 considerably narrows Black's defensive options – that said, he still has plenty of good ones to choose from.

3...d5 4 exd5

4 e5 leads to an Advance French unless Black plays 4...d4.

4...♕xd5

4...exd5 5 d4 is dealt with in Game 24, Tiviakov-Berkes. The text-move brings us back towards the subject-matter of the current chapter.

5 d4 ♘f6 *(D)*

In this game we'll look at White's attempts to develop his light-squared bishop.

6 ♗e2

6 ♗d3 leaves White well-positioned if Black takes on d4, but the problem is 6...♗e7 7 0-0 0-0, when White has no satisfactory waiting move, and after 8 c4 ♕h5 9 dxc5 ♖d8 10 ♗f4 ♕xc5 11 ♕e2 ♘c6 12 ♘c3 ♘d4 13 ♘xd4 ♕xd4 14 ♗e4 ♘xe4 15 ♘xe4 Black equalizes with the precise 15...b5! since 16 cxb5? (16 c5

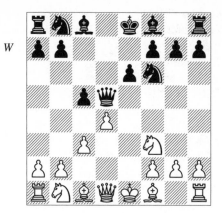

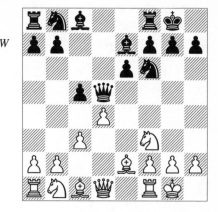

is better) 16...♗b7 17 ♖fe1 ♗b4 is bad for White.

6...♘c6

This is without question the best square for the knight, but Black has an interesting alternative. The thoughtful GM Jonathan Rowson introduced 6...cxd4 7 cxd4 ♗d7!? in the game McDonald-Rowson, British League (4NCL) 1997/8. The idea is that the light-squared bishop will generally be well-placed on c6, controlling d5 – even if it gets exchanged, Black could have interesting options of ...bxc6!?, putting the brakes on any d5 advance. The position after 8 ♘c3 ♕a5 9 0-0 ♗c6 10 ♘e5 ♗d6 11 ♗f4 ♗xe5 12 ♗xe5!? (12 dxe5 ♘d5 was assessed as equal by Rozentalis and Harley, though even here I think Black has some issues to resolve due to his b8-knight) 12...♘bd7 led to a draw in that contest (which featured 13 ♗d2), but a later game pointed to another avenue of pressure: 13 ♗d6 ♘b6 14 a4 ♘bd5 15 ♗b5 ♗xb5 16 ♘xb5 a6 17 ♘c3 ♖c8 18 ♖c1 ♘xc3 19 bxc3 ♕d5 20 ♗c5 and the black king was stuck in the centre in Vysochin-Pavlović, Cappelle la Grande 2006.

The solid 6...♗e7 7 0-0 0-0 *(D)* is also feasible, by analogy with the 6 ♗d3 variation.

This position has been extensively tested, with Sveshnikov and Pavasović taking the white pieces and the likes of Ivanchuk and Bacrot opting for Black. White can prove no more than a slight edge, if that: 8 c4 ♕d8 9 ♘c3 (9 dxc5 ♗xc5 10 ♘c3 b6 11 a3 is an edge for White, according to Rogozenko) 9...cxd4 and now White has proved nothing special after 10 ♘xd4,

while the highest level encounter here, Anand-Ivanchuk, Shenyang (World Cup) 2000, left Black with few problems holding the endgame following 10 ♕xd4 ♗d7 11 ♘e5 ♘c6 12 ♘xc6 ♗xc6 13 ♕xd8 ♖fxd8. In Pavasović's most recent game with the line, he opted for 8 ♘e5 intending 9 ♗f3, which looks like a promising alternative (it has also been tested in many games, without any firm conclusions – Black should probably refrain from the immediate capture on d4).

7 0-0 cxd4

This is far from forced, though it's easily Black's most ambitious attempt. As a player who tends to prefer piece activity over structural considerations, I'd be happy to see this were I playing White.

7...♗e7 is a much more solid move, and is the main problem with 6 ♗e2 as a winning attempt. I just don't think that White has any advantage here; for instance, 8 c4 ♕d8 9 dxc5 ♕xd1 10 ♖xd1 ♘e4 11 ♗e3 ♗xc5 12 ♘bd2 ♗xe3 13 ♘xe4 ♗f4 14 g3 ♗c7 15 ♘d6+ was Ristić-Arsović, Vrnjačka Banja 2005, and now the simplest is 15...♔e7 with level chances.

8 cxd4 ♗e7

Because White has castled, the plan with ...♗b4 is now pointless.

9 ♘c3 *(D)*

9...♕d6

This is standard, but a little more original thought could reap dividends.

9...♕a5!? was the choice of a former world junior champion, and seems a good way to avoid the main line. 10 a3 0-0 11 b4 (this was

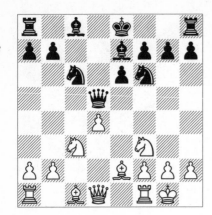

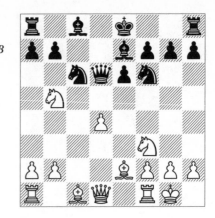

provoked by Black's previous play, but I would be amazed if such queenside expansion could be classed as a mistake – White's error comes later; Rowson suggests keeping this threat in reserve with 11 ♗e3!?) 11...♕d8 12 b5 (Rowson doesn't like this, but I think it's pretty logical – the e5-square is worth a little queenside loosening) 12...♘a5 13 ♘e5 ♗d7 14 ♗d2? (this bishop should go to a more active square) 14...♗e8 15 ♖e1 ♖c8 16 ♕a4 (Fritz suggests the ambitious 16 f4 instead) 16...a6 17 ♘a2 b6 18 ♗xa5 axb5 19 ♗xb5 bxa5 20 ♗xe8 ♖xe8 21 ♖ac1 ♖xc1 22 ♖xc1 ♕b6 23 ♘d7 ♘xd7 24 ♕xd7 ♔f8 25 ♖c8 ♖xc8 26 ♕xc8+ ♗d8 left Black with a better endgame in Gaponenko-Sutovsky, Reykjavik 2006.

9...♕d8 has also been tested in many games. Black certainly had no complaints in Cherniaev-Moiseenko, Geneva 2004: 10 ♗e3 0-0 11 ♘e5!? ♗d7 12 ♗f3 ♗e8 13 a3 ♖c8 14 ♕d2 ♘xe5 (now that White can't cleanly recapture on d1, Black goes for the queen exchange) 15 dxe5 ♕xd2 16 ♗xd2 ♘d7 17 ♗f4 ♘c5 18 ♖ad1 ♘a4 19 ♘xa4 ♗xa4 20 ♖c1 b6 and after 21 ♗e3?! ♗c2 22 ♗b7 ♖c7 23 ♖fd1 ♖d8 24 ♖xd8+ ♗xd8 25 ♗a6 ♗e4 a draw was agreed, but White has improvements, in particular 21 ♗b7!, which would have won control of the c-file, with an edge.

10 ♘b5! *(D)*

The point of this manoeuvre is to get the bishop on to the h2-b8 diagonal. White's play will mainly be on the queenside but, as we shall see, Black must always keep an eye on the centre too.

10...♕d8

This is the universal selection. At first, I thought that 10...♕b8 would be playable too, and with the bonus of preventing ♗f4, but then I found an old game and analysis by GM Jon Tisdall which cast doubt on the move: 11 g3 ♘d5 (at the board, Tisdall impressively calculated the imaginative variation 11...♗d6 12 ♘e5 ♘xd4 13 ♘xf7 ♘xe2+ 14 ♔g2 and now 14...♔xf7(?) 15 ♘xd6+ with the better game for White, but he missed that after 14...0-0! Black is OK) 12 ♗c4 a6 13 ♗xd5 axb5 14 ♗e4 with an excellent game for White, Tisdall-Fossan, Norwegian Ch, Alta 1996.

11 ♗f4

Almost universally played, but not obligatory by any means. Tisdall suggests 11 ♘e5!? a6 12 ♘xc6 bxc6 13 ♘c3 followed by ♗f3. I haven't found any high-level tests of this plan, but it looks very logical.

11...♘d5 12 ♗g3 a6

It's best to kick this guy back immediately. 12...0-0 13 ♗c4 means the b5-knight might go forward rather than back.

13 ♘c3 0-0 *(D)*

White has tried several moves here, such as 14 ♕b3, but Rublevsky selects the best option:

14 ♖c1

The rook's latent power down the c-file makes the development of the c8-bishop (with ...b6 or ...b5) more problematic.

14...♘f6

14...♘xc3 15 bxc3 b6 was chosen in Rublevsky-A.Sokolov, European Clubs Cup, St Vincent 2005. After 16 c4 ♗d6 17 ♗xd6 ♕xd6,

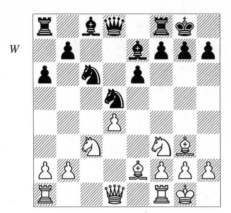

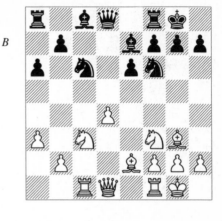

the hanging pawns didn't offer White many chances of an initiative and so Rublevsky decided to create a passed pawn with 18 c5 bxc5 19 dxc5 ♕c7 20 ♕d6 ♕xd6 21 cxd6. At first sight this looks quite dangerous for Black, who has to contend with a far-advanced passed d-pawn. Indeed, although Sokolov managed to hold, he was on the ropes for some time, and I think White has improvements, so I can't imagine anyone voluntarily aiming for such a position out of the opening. 21...♗d7 22 ♖c5 (22 ♖b1!? leaves White with a substantial advantage) 22...f6 23 ♖fc1 ♖fc8 24 ♗d1 (White is aiming for ♗a4, but Sokolov has an accurate defensive move which kills the game) 24...♘a7! 25 ♘d4 ♖xc5 26 ♖xc5 ♖c8 27 ♖xc8+ ♘xc8 28 ♘xe6 ♘xd6 (28...♗xe6 is worse: 29 ♗b3 and Black is compelled to eliminate the d-pawn, entering an inferior endgame after 29...♘xd6 30 ♗xe6+ ♔f8 31 ♔f1) 29 ♗b3 ♗c8! 30 ♔f1 ♔f7 31 ♘c7+ ♔e7 and the game was equal.

15 a3 (D)

This move is useful in stopping ...♘b4-d5, and also preparing a retreat for the light-squared bishop. Also, by waiting for one move, White prevents Black's more aggressive queenside set-up.

15 ♗c4 b5! appears very comfortable for Black.

15...b6

Preparing to complete development by fianchettoing the queen's bishop.

Of course, 15...b5 loses a pawn after 16 ♘xb5. You can see why it hasn't caught on. That said, Black has some positional compensation

after 16...axb5 17 ♖xc6 b4! 18 axb4 ♗b7 19 ♖c1 ♗xb4 20 ♕b3 ♘d5 – in such positions, it can be difficult to make anything of the extra b-pawn because Black controls so much of the b-file.

16 ♗c4

The bishop is very well placed on the a2-g8 diagonal.

16...♗b7 17 ♗a2!

This is played for two reasons. In anticipation of ...♖c8, the bishop has to move off the c-file. Also, White prepares ♕d3 and ♗b1 to attack the h7-pawn. Once Black has weakened his kingside to deal with the threats, the bishop can return to the a2-g8 diagonal.

17...♖c8 18 ♕d3 b5

18...♘h5 was played in Rublevsky-Yakovich, Russian Ch, Krasnoiarsk 2003, and Black was able to draw with precise play: 19 d5 exd5 20 ♘xd5 ♘xg3 21 hxg3 ♗f6 22 ♖fd1 ♘e5 23 ♖xc8 ♗xc8 24 ♘xe5 ♗xe5 25 ♕e3 ♗f6 26 ♖c1 ♗b7 27 ♘xf6+ ♕xf6 28 ♖c7 ♕d6! and the idea of a perpetual check on d1 and h5 secured a draw.

19 ♖fd1 (D)

White has one of the ideal IQP formations, particularly since Black hasn't managed to exchange any pieces. The following rule of thumb isn't completely accurate (not surprisingly for a rule of thumb) but still provides a reasonable guide for assessing IQP positions:

1) With four minor pieces each, White is better.

2) With two or three minor pieces each, the position is level.

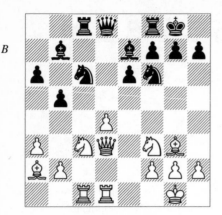 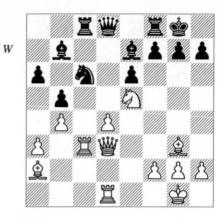

3) When only one minor piece remains on each side (or all the minor pieces have been exchanged), Black is better.

19...♞a5?

It's very risky to allow a white knight into e5. 19...b4 is Fritz's first thought, but Rogozenko points out that White has the initiative after 20 ♘a4.

20 ♞e5

This is automatic – since Black has left e5 unguarded, the white knight rushes there. Now Black must watch out for tactics on e6 and f7, as the game beautifully illustrates.

20...♞d5

Rogozenko suggests 20...♛b6 21 b4 ♞c6, though he notes that even here 22 ♘xf7!? is possible. White gets enough material, plus an attack.

21 b4 ♞xc3

21...♞c6 was the last chance, even though White has a huge advantage after 22 ♘xd5 exd5 since all of his pieces are better.

22 ♖xc3 ♞c6 (D)

Here it comes...

23 ♞xf7!

A typical blow. White immediately gets a couple of pawns, and there are more on the way.

23...♚xf7

23...♖xf7 24 ♗xe6 leaves White with a substantial initiative and approximate material equality.

24 d5!!

Shattering the remaining central defence.

24...♞a7 25 ♛xh7

Cutting Black's king off from g8.

25...♗xd5 26 ♛h5+ g6 27 ♛h7+ ♚e8 28 ♛xg6+ ♖f7 29 ♖f3

29 ♗xd5 ♖xc3 30 ♛xe6 might have been even more precise, but it's academic.

29...♗xf3 30 ♖xd8+ ♚xd8 31 gxf3 ♖f6 32 ♛e4 1-0

The queen and bishops are going to slice up the black position. Black drops more material; for instance, 32...♚e8 33 ♗e5 ♖h6 34 ♗g7 ♖h4 35 ♛g6+ ♚d8 36 ♗f6!. A vicious display by Rublevsky.

Conclusions

1) Both 6 ♗e2 and 6 ♗d3 suffer from the same defect – Black doesn't have to take on d4. With simple moves like ...♗e7 and ...0-0, I think Black can face the middlegame with confidence.

2) Assuming that Black forgets to read point 1, I think he should avoid the main line, since White obtains good pressure. It's well worth considering Sutovsky's deviation on move 9.

5 2...d5 with 4...♘f6 5 ♘f3 ♗g4 (or 5...♘c6)

1 e4 c5 2 c3 d5 3 exd5 ♕xd5 4 d4 ♘f6 5 ♘f3 ♗g4

This is the most ambitious line at Black's disposal. He develops his bishop to its best square – now, after quiet play by White, ...e6 will give Black very comfortable development.

5...♘c6 is another logical development, when White can play in similar fashion to the main line with 6 dxc5 or try the interesting 6 ♗e3. Game 18, Glavina-Moiseenko, shows some of the subtleties in these complex positions.

Now (after 5...♗g4):

6 ♗e2 used to be the main line, but I don't think it promises anything for White. He's behind in development and his pieces are more passive, factors which generally don't bode well for a vicious attack. Game 16, Stević-Areshchenko, shows how Black should handle his position.

6 dxc5 creates an interesting dilemma for Black. If he recaptures on c5, his queen will be exposed to attack. If he exchanges queens on d1, then the c5-pawn can be protected and an interesting and highly unbalanced endgame is entered. Game 17, Sermek-Chandler, is a recent game between two c3 Sicilian experts, with White getting nothing.

Game 16
Hrvoje Stević – Alexander Areshchenko
European Ch, Warsaw 2005

1 e4 c5 2 c3 d5 3 exd5 ♕xd5 4 d4 ♘f6 5 ♘f3 ♗g4 *(D)*

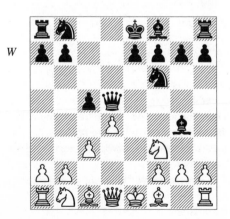

W

6 ♗e2

This is the traditional main line, but Black has never been particularly worried. 6 dxc5 is much more interesting. White also has some innocuous alternatives:

a) 6 ♕a4+ ♗d7 7 ♕b3 cxd4 8 ♘xd4 ♘c6 9 ♗e3 ♘a5 10 ♕xd5 ♘xd5 11 ♗c1 e5 leaves Black with a very comfortable endgame.

b) 6 ♘bd2 aims to hold a bunch of squares, but one knight can only do so much. After 6...♘c6 7 ♗c4 ♗xf3 8 ♕b3 ♘a5 9 ♕b5+ ♕d7 10 ♘xf3 ♘xc4 11 ♕xc4 cxd4 12 ♘xd4 e6 the tactical sequence has fizzled out and the resulting position is level.

6...e6

The natural move, preparing to develop the bishop and castle while protecting the c5-pawn.

After the careless 6...♘c6, for instance, 7 dxc5! gives White a favourable version of the 6 dxc5 lines, since his queen won't be displaced in the event of an exchange on d1 while 7...♕xc5 8 ♗e3 ♕a5 9 ♕b3 ♕c7 10 ♘a3 looks like an edge.

7 h3

Putting the question to the bishop is useful, for two reasons:

1) White now has the option of generating kingside play with g4 – most of the time, this isn't a particularly bright idea, but sometimes it can be helpful.

2) White avoids any potential back-rank tactics when he castles, since the h2-square is available for the king.

7...♗h5 (D)

Of course, capturing on f3 is out of the question since the white bishop would be dominant on the long diagonal.

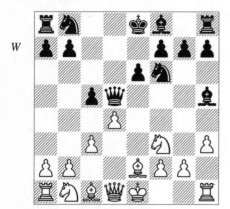

8 0-0

Castling is always the most natural move, and here it has the added benefit of side-stepping any ideas based on ...♗b4+ (after an exchange on d4).

8 c4 is the alternative plan: 8...♕d8 9 ♘c3 cxd4 10 ♘xd4 ♗xe2 11 ♕a4+!? (neither plausible recapture on e2 offers anything, but this move tries to keep the game alive) 11...♘bd7 (11...♕d7 12 ♕xd7+ ♘bxd7 13 ♔xe2 looks level) 12 ♘dxe2 ♗e7 13 0-0 0-0 14 ♕c2. Rozentalis and Harley like this for White, but it looks pretty level; for instance, 14...♖c8 15 b3 a6 and Black has ideas like ...♕a5 or ...b5.

8...♘c6

Black brings another piece to its best square and puts pressure on the d-pawn. It's interesting

that Black has completely developed his queenside, but has two more moves to make before his kingside development is taken care of, while White is in the opposite situation. When delaying the development of one's kingside, the main factor to consider is how easy it will be for the opponent to open a central file, and here White has few chances of generating anything meaningful on the e-file before Black castles.

9 ♗e3 (D)

By threatening to take on c5, White encourages Black to capture the d-pawn which, in turn, will free the c3-square for the white knight.

9 a3 was an idea of Nigel Short's, remaining flexible with the placement of the queen's bishop, though after 9...cxd4 (9...♗e7 isn't too great, since the bishop will lose a tempo if it takes on c5, while 10 c4 ♕d8 11 dxc5 ♕xd1 12 ♖xd1 a5 13 ♗e3 ♘e4 14 ♘bd2 ♘xc5 15 b4! gives White an edge) 10 cxd4 ♗e7 11 ♘c3 ♕d6 it's not clear that White has anything better than 12 ♗e3 since 12 ♘b5 ♕b8 doesn't trouble Black.

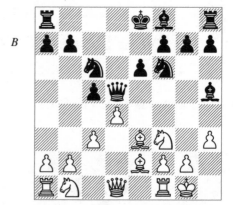

9...cxd4

While this gives the c3-square to the knight, it is Black's best move for two reasons:

1) It is more or less forced (otherwise dxc5 will win a pawn);

2) White has played his bishop to an inferior square, so this will be quite a playable IQP position for Black.

It's also comforting for Black that his light-squared bishop is outside the pawn-chain. This dramatically reduces White's chances of a kingside attack, since Black will always have ...♗xf3 or ...♗g6 to exchange some pieces. However, the black queenside is slightly weakened by the bishop's departure, so it makes sense for White to seek play on this side of the board.

10 cxd4 ♗e7

Clearly the best square for the bishop – it wouldn't be well placed on d6 (blocking Black's pressure down the d-file), plus Black wants the d6-square for his queen.

11 ♘c3

Natural and best.

11...♕d6 (D)

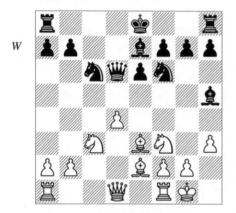

As mentioned before, White finds it difficult to generate anything on the kingside, since his pieces are rather passive and Black's light-squared bishop is an excellent defender. Therefore he aims for the alternative plan of playing on the queenside.

12 ♕b3

Putting pressure on b7, but it will take some more preparation before this becomes a genuine threat.

12...0-0!

Black can have very few complaints about such a position.

13 ♖fd1

Of course, 13 ♕xb7? ♖ab8 14 ♕a6 ♖xb2 is very nice for Black.

13...♘b4

This is a typical manoeuvre, with the idea of solidly blockading the d-pawn. However, there

is nothing wrong with the alternative, namely attacking the d-pawn with 13...♖fd8. This is more ambitious and complex than the game continuation.

14 ♗g5 ♘bd5!

Often the problem with this knight manoeuvre is that the e5-square is left open to a white knight (which can combine with a rook on e1 and a bishop on the a2-g8 diagonal to generate play against the e6- and f7-pawns – see Game 15, Rublevsky-Vitiugov, for a model demonstration of such a plan), but here Black doesn't have such concerns – there's no white rook on the e-file, and instead of being actively placed on a2, b3 or c4, the bishop is stuck on e2. In addition, the f3-knight is effectively pinned.

15 ♗xf6!?

An atypical operation, but not a bad one. The resulting position just looks like a draw, which is as much as White can hope for in such a position. After something like 15 ♖ac1 ♖fd8 it's hard to suggest an active plan for White.

15...♗xf6 (D)

This is clearly the right recapture. 15...♘xf6 16 d5 exd5 17 ♘xd5 slightly favours White, as he will be the first to occupy the central files.

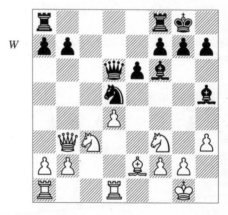

16 ♘xd5

White consistently continues his plan. 16 ♘e4? is misguided in view of 16...♕f4 17 ♘xf6+ ♕xf6 – Black has excellent chances in such a simplified IQP position.

16...exd5

Now both sides have an isolated d-pawn. These pawns are therefore immune to frontal attack but can be reached by the minor pieces. There is a slight material imbalance in that Black has a dark-squared bishop for a knight, but the position is equal since in such structures knights are the full equivalent of bishops. Moreover, as mentioned at move 16, should the balance get down to one knight vs one bishop, I think White should fancy his chances.

16...♕xd5 17 ♕xd5 exd5 18 g4 ♗g6 19 ♗d3 leaves White with reasonable grinding chances. In such structures I think a knight outperforms a lone bishop since it can both defend its own d-pawn and attack the opponent's.

17 ♖d2

White is creating some pressure on the d5- and b7-pawns. Areshchenko now makes the correct decision to sacrifice one and enter a dead endgame:

17...♖fe8! 18 ♕xb7

Consenting to what's coming, but there is nothing better.

18...♖eb8

Of course 18...♗xf3 19 ♗xf3 ♖eb8 fails to 20 ♕xd5.

19 ♕a6 ♕xa6 20 ♗xa6 ♗xf3 21 gxf3 ♖b6 22 ♗f1 a5 23 f4 ½-½

Opposite-coloured bishops have strongly drawish tendencies in endgames, and Black will have no problem holding this one, so Stević saw no point in playing on.

Conclusions

1) 5...♗g4 is, in many ways, Black's most natural continuation. He puts his bishop on its best square, and continues to exert pressure on the white d-pawn.

2) I don't believe in any of White's 6th-move options covered in this game. They all allow Black easy development.

3) While an IQP normally gives considerable attacking chances, this isn't the case when Black can get his bishop to g4, since this piece can drop back to g6 and neutralize anything White generates on the b1-h7 diagonal.

Game 17

Dražen Sermek – Murray Chandler

New Zealand open Ch, Queenstown 2006

1 e4 c5 2 c3 d5 3 exd5 ♕xd5 4 d4 ♘f6 5 ♘f3 ♗g4 6 dxc5 *(D)*

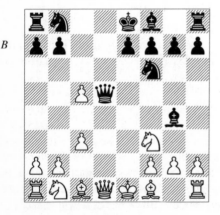

This approach has rekindled interest in the whole c3 Sicilian. White had major problems demonstrating any advantage after other moves,

but now he forces play into unbalanced and original channels. Black has a choice:

1) He can take on d1, after which he will try to use his initiative to put pressure on the under-developed white position;

2) He can take on c5, restoring material equality, but leaving his queen as a target.

The jury is still out on which approach is best, but my personal opinion is that 6...♕xc5, when well handled, is most likely to yield equality.

6...♕xd1+

White's king will now be stuck in the centre. There is a general principle that 'the king is well placed in the centre in the endgame', but this position is much more of a queenless middlegame than an endgame – only the queens have been exchanged. While the king is unlikely to get mated (though it can happen), the main problems with his position are these:

1) Black can gain time for development – ...♘c6 and ...0-0-0+ is an obvious example, but depending on where the king moves, ideas like ...♗f5(+) frequently enter the position.

2) The white pieces can find themselves tied down to inferior squares. For instance, if White blocks a check on the d-file by playing ♘(b)d2, both of his knights will be pinned (one by a rook on d8, the other by a bishop on g4). These pieces would be much more effective on c4 and e5, but won't be able to get there without some groundwork.

A recent and typical high-level game involving 6...♕xc5 ended in a draw: 7 ♘a3! (this is the most flexible move) 7...a6! (Black has tried alternatives with varying success, but I think that leaving ♘b5 in the pipeline is more trouble than it's worth) 8 ♗e3 ♕c7 9 h3 ♗h5 10 g4 ♗g6 11 ♗g2 (D).

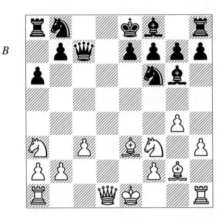

There's something very logical about this gain of space and easy development, but of course weaknesses are also created by such play. In particular, Black doesn't have to lose control of the centre, and as long as he has some good squares there he has little to fear. 11...♘bd7! (a smart development, allowing ...0-0-0 and not letting White bring her knight into play via c4) 12 g5 ♘e4 13 ♘h4 ♘d6 (this knight is extremely well placed for defensive purposes) 14 ♘xg6 hxg6 15 ♘c2 0-0-0 16 ♕e2 ♘f5 (a perfect square for the knight) 17 0-0-0 (castling kingside would have entailed a lot of risk, so Kosteniuk goes for the safer option) 17...e6 18 ♔b1 ♗e7 19 ♘b4 (she could also have retained

the bishop by retreating to c1, though the knight on f5 is at least as good a piece) 19...♘xe3 20 ♕xe3 ♘b6 21 ♘d3 ♘d5 22 ♕e5 ♕xe5 23 ♘xe5 (White has some pressure on f7, but Black can easily handle it) 23...♘f4! 24 ♖xd8+ ♖xd8 25 ♗e4 ♖d2! (now the game degenerates into a draw) 26 ♘xf7 ♖xf2 27 h4 ♖e2 28 ♗f3 ♖f2 29 ♗e4 ♖e2 30 ♗f3 ♖f2 31 ♗e4 ½-½ Kosteniuk-Bu Xiangzhi, Moscow (Aeroflot Open) 2006.

7 ♔xd1 e5!

Other moves are distinctly dubious. This one creates two threats – to a pawn (...♗xc5) and to a piece (...e4). Oddly enough, it's the pawn that White should be worried about.

8 b4! *(D)*

Black would have an advantage if he could play ...♗xc5.

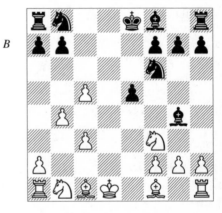

8...e4

Not quite winning a piece, due to the following simple tactical device (also known from the Botvinnik Semi-Slav):

9 h3 ♗h5

The bishop has to stay on this diagonal. There's no value in 9...♗xf3+ 10 gxf3 exf3 since Black has an inferior pawn-structure and no active play, while White's two bishops will be very effective. The simplest plan is 11 ♗c4, intending 12 ♖e1+ to nudge the black king away from the f7-pawn.

10 g4

Breaking the pin, but Black has a trick of his own.

10...♘xg4! 11 hxg4 ♗xg4

Not only is Black regaining his piece, but he threatens to grab a whole rook, which restricts White's possible responses.

12 ᐃd2

By far the safest move, and one which remains flexible with the development of the f1-bishop.

12 ᐃc2 is a definite mistake, since it allows Black to take on f3 with the bishop: 12...ᐃxf3 and Black's structure is perfect.

12...h5!? (D)

This is a twist on the old lines. It's obviously useful to start running with the h-pawn, and Black wants White to commit his f1-bishop. Instead, 12...exf3 13 ᐃd3 allows White to bring his bishop to the excellent e4-square.

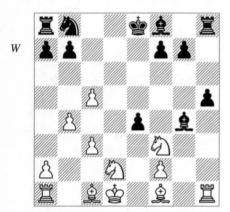

13 ᐃh3

An interesting attempt, but I'm not convinced that this is the strongest move.

13 ᐃc2 had been tested in some previous encounters. 13...exf3 14 ᐃc4!? (I find this move instructive: the f3-pawn is small fry, so instead of devoting time to its capture, White accelerates his queenside play) 14...ᐃc6 and now:

a) 15 ᐃf4 ᐃe6 16 a4 ᐃe7 17 a5 a6 18 ᐃe1 ᐃf8 19 ᐃb6 ᐃd8 20 ᐃh3 ᐃxh3 21 ᐃxh3 g5 22 ᐃc7 g4 23 ᐃxd8 was agreed drawn in Alekseev-Loginov, St Petersburg 2000 – if we continue a little, 23...ᐃxd8 24 ᐃd7+ ᐃg7 25 ᐃg1 ᐃg5! 26 ᐃxf3 gxf3 27 ᐃxg5+ ᐃh6 28 ᐃg3 h4 29 ᐃg4 h3 30 ᐃh4+ ᐃg7 31 ᐃg4+ forces a cute perpetual check.

b) 15 ᐃd3 0-0-0 16 ᐃf4 f6 17 a4 g5 18 ᐃh2! (D).

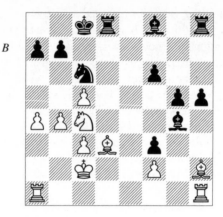

The black kingside pawns have trouble advancing, while the white queenside pawns are gaining some extremely useful space. Note that the bishop on g4 is badly placed, which is some justification for not playing to win the f3-pawn and forcing a bishop exchange. 18...f5 19 b5 ᐃb8 20 ᐃd6+ ᐃxd6 21 ᐃxd6 ᐃhe8 22 ᐃae1 (the extra pawn is cold comfort to Black – he's just losing on the queenside) 22...ᐃd7 23 c6 ᐃxe1 24 cxb7+ ᐃxb7 25 ᐃxe1 ᐃf6 (25...ᐃb6 is very strongly met by 26 ᐃe7+ ᐃa8 27 ᐃe5, since 28 a5 follows) 26 ᐃe6 ᐃe4 27 ᐃe7+ ᐃa8 28 ᐃe5! and the white bishops were dominant in Deviatkin-Krapivin, St Petersburg 2005 – note that 28...ᐃxf2? 29 ᐃc4 leads to a mating attack.

13...ᐃxh3

This exchange should be automatic. Naturally, 13...ᐃxf3+?? 14 ᐃxf3 exf3 would be an horrendous positional decision, even without the crushing 15 ᐃc8!.

14 ᐃxh3

Not a nice square for the rook – it presents a handy target for Black's pawn advance. This is the main reason I prefer 13 ᐃc2.

14...exf3 (D)

15 ᐃxf3

I know I'm complaining about the rook on h3, but 15 ᐃxf3? would be incorrect – the rook has to stay on the h-file to block the pawn. After 15...h4 16 ᐃh3 ᐃc6 White has nice squares for his knight on c4 or e4, but I doubt whether this slight improvement on the f3-square is worth the two tempi it costs.

15...ᐃc6

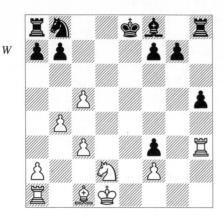

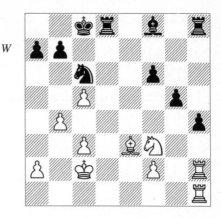

Natural, and quite probably best. An argument can also be made for 15...♘d7, when it is harder for White to execute the b5 advance.

16 ♗e3 f6!

Correct – Black plays for ...g5 rather than ...g6. He has to push his kingside pawns.

17 ♔c2 g5

This illustrates one of the major problems with a rook on h3 – Black threatens to win a piece already. When White is forced to undertake defensive moves on the kingside, it's a bad sign.

18 ♖h2

18 ♘d4 is the alternative method of dealing with the threatened ...g4.

18...0-0-0 19 ♖ah1

It's more normal for White to play on the queenside in these lines. Sermek has an interesting piece sacrifice in mind, but it's just a draw.

19 b5 ♘e7 20 ♗d4 ♖h6 21 a4 would be the 'race' alternative – as always, these positions are extremely difficult to judge. In this particular version, I'd prefer White, but I find it hard to explain why! If he can get his king to c4 and start pushing his a-pawn, I think Black will be in trouble.

19...h4 *(D)*

20 ♘xg5

Without this, it's very hard to make sense of the white kingside configuration. 20 a4 is a more standard continuation, aiming to race, but the white rooks look awful in this situation.

20...fxg5 21 ♗xg5 ♗e7

Black can try to keep more tension with 21...♖e8, but this just gives White chances after

22 f4, when his bishop and rooks could combine effectively against the black king.

22 ♗xe7 ♘xe7 23 ♖xh4 ♖xh4 24 ♖xh4

White runs no major risk of losing this after eliminating the last black kingside pawn, but his winning chances aren't so hot either. Personally, I'd take Black.

24...♖f8 25 f4 ♘d5

This wins the f-pawn, but I doubt that Sermek thought he could hold on to this in any event.

26 ♖h5! ♘xf4 27 ♖h7

It's important for White to keep the rooks on, since otherwise there would be a very real risk of zugzwang,

27...♘d5 28 ♔d3 ♖f3+ 29 ♔c4 ♘f6

29...♘e3+ doesn't seem to give Black much either.

30 ♖g7 ♘d7 31 a4 ♔c7 32 b5 ♖f4+ 33 ♔d5 ♖f5+

After 33...♖xa4, 34 b6+! draws.

34 ♔d4 ♖f4+ 35 ♔d5 ♖f5+ 36 ♔d4 ♖f4+ ½-½

Neither side has any winning chances, since everything's on one side of the board. The best Black can hope for is a drawn rook + knight vs rook position, and I doubt that he can even get that.

Conclusions

1) 6 dxc5 is White's best winning attempt after 5...♗g4. The resulting positions are highly unbalanced and quite original, which means a well-prepared player can pick up a lot of points here.

2) Black's choice between 6...♕xc5 and 6...♕xd1+ is not an easy one. Personally, I think 6...♕xc5 gives better chances of equalizing quickly, but Black must play precisely for several moves. Kosteniuk-Bu Xiangzhi (in the note to Black's 6th move) is illustrative of what he should be aiming for.

3) In the endgame after 6...♕xd1+, Black goes a pawn up in the main line. However, he needs to be very careful in handing the white queenside majority. I recommend 12...h5 in order to prevent White's bishop from getting to e4.

4) I don't like Sermek's 13 ♗h3. 13 ♔c2 is a much better winning attempt.

Game 18

Pablo Glavina Rossi – Alexander Moiseenko
Spanish Team Ch, Sanxenxo 2004

1 e4 c5 2 ♘f3 ♘c6 3 c3 d5 4 exd5 ♕xd5 5 d4 ♘f6 *(D)*

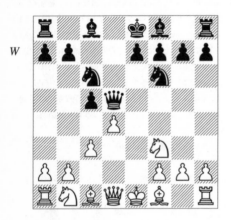

W

6 dxc5!?

This is critical, with similar play to Game 17, Sermek-Chandler.

6 ♗e3 is a major alternative. If Black takes on d4, play will transpose into common IQP positions, which are often reached via the move-order 1 e4 c5 2 c3 d5 3 exd5 ♕xd5 4 d4 ♘f6 5 ♘f3 e6 6 ♗e3 cxd4 7 cxd4 ♘c6. 6...♘g4 is the main attempt to get away from these positions. After 7 ♘bd2 ♘xe3 (7...cxd4 8 ♗c4 is nice for White, since 8...♘xe3 9 fxe3! gives him a menacing lead in development) 8 fxe3, Black has the bishop-pair but White has a strong centre and easy development. Overall, one would have to regard these positions as a little better for White. Gallagher-Arakhamia, Gibraltar 2004 is a case in point: 8...e6 9 ♗d3 ♗e7 10 ♕c2! (now Black will have to waste

some time before she can castle) 10...♗d7 11 0-0 ♕h5 12 ♘e4 cxd4 13 exd4 0-0 14 b4!. White has an advantage in all areas of the board, while the black bishops haven't made their presence felt. White is also better after 6...e5 7 dxe5 ♕xd1+ 8 ♔xd1 ♗g4 9 ♘a3!.

6...♕xd1+

Entering the endgame – this would definitely be my choice with the black pieces. He gets interesting compensation in the resulting position. 6...♕xc5 *(D)* is the alternative.

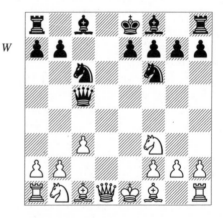

W

After 7 ♘a3, Black's main attempt seems to be 7...♘g4, which looks very artificial to me: 8 ♕e2 ♗f5 (Black should probably play 8...a6) 9 h3 ♘f6 10 ♗e3 ♕a5 11 ♘c4 ♕c7 12 0-0-0 (this is indicative of White's prospects in this line – he has brought his bishop and knight into the game with tempo, and now prevents Black from castling) 12...e6 13 g3! (it's common to play g4 in such positions, but now ♗f4 is a threat)

13...♖d8 14 ♗g2 ♘d5 15 ♘d4 ♘xe3 16 ♘b5 ♕b8 17 ♕xe3 ♗e7 18 ♗xc6+ bxc6 19 ♖xd8+ ♕xd8 20 ♖d1 ♕xd1+ 21 ♔xd1 cxb5 was Collins-R.Pert, British League (4NCL) 2003/4, which I won but, as my opponent pointed out, I could have forced resignation here with 22 ♕xa7! in view of 22...bxc4 23 ♕a4+! and 24 ♕a8+, winning the rook.

7 ♔xd1 e5

I'm sure this move is best – Black threatens the c5-pawn and gains some useful central control. In addition, the advance ...e4 is a constant threat.

7...♗f5 at once is also logical. White's best idea is probably 8 ♗e3 0-0-0+ 9 ♔c1, tucking the king away on the queenside.

7...♘g4 is a shot in the dark. There's nothing wrong with 8 ♗e3, but the fact that the knight has already committed itself justifies 8 ♔e1, when Black will struggle to show enough for the pawn. It's worth mentioning that Black has to play quite precisely in these ...♕xd1+ lines, since he can easily find himself a pawn down for nothing in the endgame.

8 b4 (D)

As always, letting Black take on c5 isn't a realistic option.

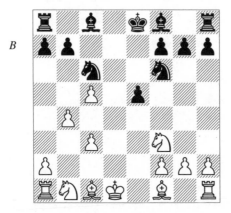

Black has some interesting compensation for the pawn in this position. He doesn't have time to set up the ...♗g4 and ...e4 idea, but his alternative plans include cutting off the white king with ...♗f5, and playing aggressively on the queenside with ...a5.

8...♗f5

Cutting the white king off from the c2-square, while increasing the lead in development to threatening proportions.

8...♗g4 is another idea. However, the only real point of this move is to take on f3, which weakens the white structure but gives up an important minor piece, and leaves White with the two bishops on an open board. 9 ♔c2! is clearly the way to start – White side-steps the pin and takes advantage of the fact that ...♗f5+ will rarely be an efficient use of Black's time. Now I haven't found any clear route to equality for Black: 9...a5 (pure piece-play is unconvincing: 9...0-0-0 10 ♗e3 ♘d5 11 ♗b5 ♗xf3 12 gxf3 a5 13 ♗xc6 bxc6 14 a3 f5 15 c4 ♘c7 16 f4 and White was starting to consolidate in Nadyrkhanov-Maiorov, Krasnodar 2001) 10 ♗b5 (not 10 b5 ♗xf3 11 gxf3 ♘d8, when White can't hold his c5-pawn) 10...axb4 (10...♗xf3 11 gxf3 axb4 12 cxb4 ♘d5 13 ♗d2 leaves White a healthy pawn up) 11 ♘xe5 ♗f5+ and now, rather than the 12 ♗d3? b3+! of Baklan-Mikhalets, Alushta 1998, the white king should go forward. After 12 ♔b3 ♗e6+ 13 c4 Black is in trouble.

We now return to 8...♗f5 (D):

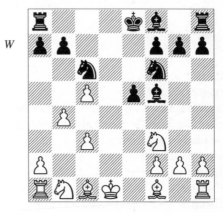

9 ♗c4

While this move is obviously a desirable one, it doesn't address the main problem in the position. Black is about to castle queenside, and White needs to decide where he should place his king.

9 ♗e3 frees the c1-square for the king. Now that the sting has been drawn from ...0-0-0+,

Black should search for compensation elsewhere. 9...♘d5 and now:

a) 10 ♗c4 0-0-0 11 ♔c1 ♗e7 was agreed drawn in Cherniaev-M.Röder, Zaragoza 1997, but I'd take White here. I'm sceptical of Black's ability to generate full compensation in the lines where he omits ...a5, since the white queenside pawns control a lot of key squares.

b) 10 ♔c1 a5! (an excellent attempt to seek compensation) 11 b5 (White wins the e5-pawn, but a lot of his position falls apart in return) 11...♘d8 12 ♘xe5 ♘xe3 13 fxe3 ♗xc5 14 ♗c4 (14 ♘c4 a4 leaves Black with excellent compensation – he follows with the simple 15...♖c8) 14...♗xe3+ 15 ♔b2 0-0 (D) leads to an unusual endgame.

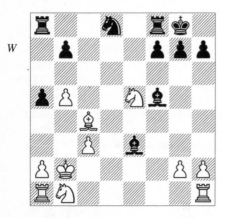

The main factor, in my opinion, is not Black's bishop-pair (...♗e6, to exchange and get the knight into the game, is a common occurrence anyway) but the white queenside majority. It is well-advanced and controls some important squares, but c5 is now an outpost and, with ...b6, Black could prevent White from generating a passed pawn (unless the b6-pawn drops). After 16 ♖f1 ♗e6 17 ♘a3 ♗c5 18 ♖ad1 ♖c8 19 ♗xe6 ♗xa3+ 20 ♔xa3 ♘xe6 21 c4 we reach a position that has been tested in a couple of games. After 21...f6 22 ♘d7 ♖fe8 23 ♘b6 ♖b8 24 ♔a4 White won the a-pawn in Rausis-Wirthensohn, 2nd Bundesliga 1990/1, so Nadyrkhanov's suggestion, 21...♘c5, looks like the best move. The analysis runs 22 ♘d7 ♖fe8 23 ♘xc5 ♖xc5 24 ♖d7 ♖xc4, which Rogozenko and Harley think will peter out to a draw, but in

fact it's an extremely difficult endgame. After a natural sequence like 25 ♖xb7 ♖e3+ 26 ♔b2 ♖e2+ 27 ♔b3 ♖b4+ 28 ♔c3 f6 Black is very active, but the b5-pawn is a huge asset.

The endgames arising in these dxc5 ♕xd1+ lines can be quite sharp, and this is well illustrated by the fact that Sermek lost a miniature here: 9 ♗b5 0-0-0+ 10 ♔e2?! (the king isn't safe on the e-file; I'd prefer 10 ♘bd2, but Black still looks very comfortable) 10...♗e7 11 ♗e3 ♘d5 12 ♗xc6 bxc6 13 ♘xe5 ♖he8 14 ♘xf7 ♘xe3 15 ♘xd8? (15 fxe3 is better) 15...♘c4 16 ♘xc6 ♗f6+?! (missing a beautiful win by 16...♗h4+ 17 ♔f3 ♗e4+! 18 ♔g4 ♗xf2! and the white king is in a mating-net) 17 ♔d1 (White had to try 17 ♔f3, though the position after 17...♗e4+ 18 ♔g3 ♗xc6 appears promising for Black) 17...♘b2+ 18 ♔c1 ♘d3+ 19 ♔c2 ♘xb4++ 20 ♔b3 ♘xc6 21 ♘a3 ♖e7 22 ♘b5 ♖b7 23 a4 a6 24 c4 ♘d4+ 0-1 Sermek-Wirthensohn, Bad Wörishofen 1993.

We now return to 9 ♗c4 (D):

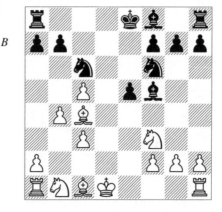

9...a5!

Now that White doesn't have ♗b5, this is the most natural plan.

9...0-0-0+ looks counterintuitive, since the f7-pawn is going to drop off and Black hasn't started his queenside counterplay yet (also, it is useful to have a rook on the a-file so that, after ...a5, a3 axb4, the a3-pawn is pinned). Though Black managed to draw in Schmittdiel-Donaldson, Liechtenstein 1994, his position was awful after 10 ♔e2 ♗e7 11 ♘g5 ♖hf8 12 ♘xf7 ♖d7, when simply 13 ♖d1 would have left Black with enough compensation for one pawn, but not two.

10 b5

This isn't the move White wants to make, but he has to. 10 a3? axb4 11 cxb4 ♘g4 and 12...♘xb4 isn't so hot for White.

10...0-0-0+

This leaves the f7-pawn vulnerable, but is a key component in the following tactical sequence.

11 ♔e1 e4! *(D)*

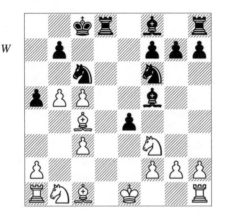

Now if the f3-knight moves, Black can play ...♘e5.

12 bxc6

This is just good for Black, but White already has problems.

12 ♘g5 ♘e5 13 ♗xf7 lands White in trouble after the superb 13...♔d7!!, simply threatening ...h6 without allowing ♗e6+. After 14 c6+ (there's nothing better for White) 14...bxc6 15 bxc6+ ♔xc6 16 ♗e6 ♗g6 Black follows up by ...♘d3+ and ...♗c5, with a beautiful position. The pawn deficit is irrelevant, since the f2-pawn will fall in a few moves.

12...exf3 13 cxb7+

13 gxf3 bxc6 cuts the black king off from the c5-pawn, but it doesn't matter because 14 ♗e3 ♘d7 15 ♘d2 ♗xc5 16 ♗xf7 ♗d6 still leaves superb compensation in view of ...♘e5.

13...♔xb7

Now White has a fairly grim choice to make.

14 ♗e3

14 gxf3 leaves White with one of the worst pawn-structures you're likely to come across.

After 14...♗xc5 15 ♗xf7 ♖hf8 16 ♗b3 ♖fe8+ 17 ♗e3 ♗xe3 18 fxe3 ♖xe3+ 19 ♔f2 Black can regain the material immediately with 19...♖xf3+ 20 ♔xf3 ♗e4+, but it's much better to retain superb compensation with 19...♖de8. If White wants to hold on to the c3-pawn, the b1-knight (and, in turn, the a1-rook) won't be going anywhere.

14...fxg2 15 ♖g1 ♘g4 16 ♗d4 *(D)*

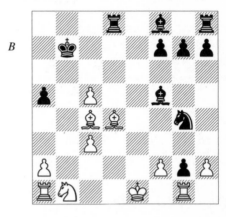

It's understandable that White wanted to keep this bishop, but Black can exchange it in any event. The g4-knight also has some promising attacking options.

16...♗e7?!

The first slip from Moiseenko. 16...♔c6! is the move Black wants to play, since the bishop should land on c5, not e7. White is in major difficulties here; for instance, 17 ♖xg2 ♗xc5 18 ♗xc5 ♔xc5 and 19...♖he8 is in the post.

17 ♖xg2 ♗f6 18 ♘d2 ♖he8+ *(D)*

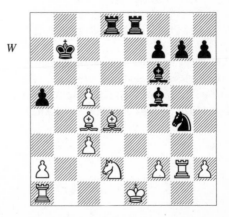

19 ♔f1

19 ♔d1?? just loses to 19...♗xd4 20 cxd4 ♖xd4, when the black attack is too strong.

19...♗xd4 20 cxd4 ♖xd4 21 ♗b5

21 ♘b3!? is a cute trick. There are no tricks based on an exchange sacrifice on c4 followed by ...♗d3+ since the g4-knight hangs. However, Black still has some advantage after 21...♖f4 22 ♖e1 ♖xe1+ 23 ♔xe1 a4 24 ♗d5+ ♔c7.

21...♖e7 22 ♖e1 ♖xe1+ 23 ♔xe1 g6 (D)

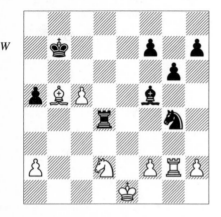

This is a difficult endgame. Overall, I'd take Black, since his pieces are more active and he has fewer formal weaknesses. However, the c5-pawn could be a major asset.

24 f3 ♘e5 25 ♖e2 f6 26 ♖e3?

Going for a loose formation – the king isn't well placed on e2, since it can't cover the h-pawn.

26 ♔f2 is better, as then the king can move to the g-file to cover the h-pawn when it's attacked. The position after 26...♖b4 27 a4 ♘d3+ 28 ♔g3 ♘xc5 29 ♘c4! is completely unclear.

26...a4 27 ♔e2 ♖b4 28 ♗e8 ♔c7 29 a3 ♖h4 (D)

Now Black has a serious advantage, since all the white pawns are potential weaknesses.

30 ♘e4 ♖xh2+ 31 ♔d1 ♖h1+ 32 ♔e2 ♖h2+ 33 ♔d1 ♖h1+ 34 ♔e2 ♗xe4 35 ♖xe4 ♖h2+ 36

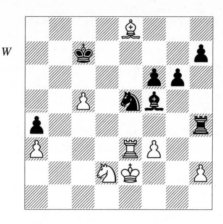

♔f1 ♘xf3 37 ♖xa4 ♘d2+ 38 ♔e1 ♘f3+ 39 ♔f1 ♖b2 40 c6 ♘e5 41 ♖a7+ ♔d6 42 ♖xh7 g5 43 ♖a7 ♖b8 44 ♗d7 ♖b6 45 ♔e2 ♘xc6 46 ♗xc6 ♖xc6 47 ♔e3 ♔e6 48 a4 ♔f5

This endgame is an easy win, since the connected passed pawns provide shelter for the black king.

49 a5 ♔g4 50 ♖b7 f5 51 ♖b4+ f4+ 52 ♔e4 ♖e6+ 53 ♔d4 ♔g3 54 ♖a4 ♖a6 55 ♖a1 ♖a8 0-1

Conclusions

1) Bringing out both knights simply can't be a bad idea for Black. In reply, White has a major decision to make. I think my choice would be 6 ♗e3, when White gets a decent IQP position if Black takes on d4, while the lines after 6...♘g4 seem to leave White with a solid edge.

2) 6 dxc5 leads to similar positions to the previous game, but there are subtle differences. I recommend that Black takes on d1, when his omission of ...♗g4 means that he can't force through ...e5-e4, but he gains a range of alternative options. His best ones all include ...a5 at some point. I recommend 8...♗f5. After this, I really think 9 ♗c4 a5! is just good for Black, so White should play 9 ♗e3, but even this line doesn't look too scary for Black.

6 2...d5: Alternatives to 4...♘f6

1 e4 c5 2 c3 d5 3 exd5 ♕xd5 4 d4

Black needn't rush with 4...♘f6. In all the lines in this chapter, there are many possible transpositions based on a later ...♘f6, but there are also some promising independent options.

4...♘c6

Creating immediate pressure on the d-pawn – indeed, Black is threatening to capture it.

4...g6 is one of the more ambitious defences for Black in the c3 Sicilian – the bishop will be excellently placed on the a1-h8 diagonal. Game 21, Sermek-Cebalo, is a good illustration of the concepts.

5 ♘f3

Developing and defending the d-pawn. Now:

5...♗g4 re-establishes the threat. Game 19, Nayer-Lautier, shows some excellent preparation by the French GM, which seriously threatens White's attempts for an edge.

5...cxd4 leads to independent options – Black can play against the d-pawn or try for ...♗b4, while White has the option of ♘c3. Game 20, Al Sayed-Adly, shows some of the details.

Game 19
Evgeny Nayer – Joël Lautier
FIDE World Cup, Khanty-Mansiisk 2005

The French GM Joël Lautier has made important contributions to a wide range of openings, both as a player and as a second. In this game, he completely neutralizes a line which had previously caused some problems for Black.

1 e4 c5 2 ♘f3 ♘c6 3 c3 d5 4 exd5 ♕xd5 5 d4 ♗g4 *(D)*

5...♘f6 was covered in Game 18, Glavina-Moiseenko.

6 ♗e2

This is the most natural move, breaking the pin.

6...cxd4

Isolating the white d-pawn at the cost of freeing the c3-square for White's queen's knight.

Black can also play the immediate 6...e6, which prevents ♘c3 for the moment but gives White options of hitting the queen with c4.

7 cxd4 e6 8 ♘c3

Now Black has a choice.

8...♕a5

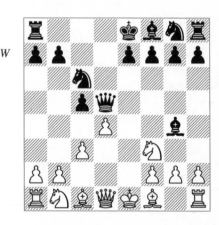

He decides to bring the queen to safety and pin the c3-knight.

8...♗b4 9 0-0 ♕a5 *(D)* is the alternative.

Then 10 h3 ♗xf3 (10...♗h5 11 ♗e3 ♘ge7 12 ♕b3 0-0 13 a3 ♗xc3 14 bxc3 slightly favoured White in Pavasović-V.Georgiev, Turin Olympiad 2006) 11 ♗xf3 ♘ge7 (11...♗xc3 12

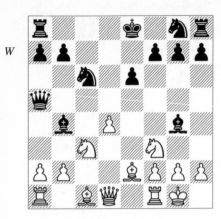

W

bxc3 ♛xc3 13 ♗g5 followed by d5 is superb for White) 12 ♗e3 0-0 13 ♛b3 ♖fd8 14 a3 ♗xc3 15 bxc3 ♛c7 16 ♗g5 ♖d7 left Black with a reasonable position in Papaioannou-Cheparinov, European Team Ch, Gothenburg 2005.

9 h3

This is the critical continuation, putting the question to the bishop.

9...♗h5

This retreat maintains the pressure. 9...♗xf3 10 ♗xf3 ♖d8 looks like a decent alternative, since Black creates substantial pressure on the d-pawn. That said, the f3-bishop is a massive piece.

10 d5!? (D)

This pawn sacrifice has been the main attempt to upset Black. It was introduced by Joel Benjamin a couple of decades ago. Instead, 10 0-0 ♘f6 11 ♗e3 ♗d6! leaves Black with fair activity and the better structure – I don't think White can be better here.

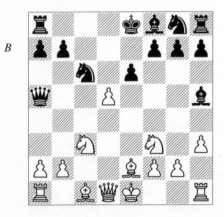

B

10...exd5

This is not forced.

10...♖d8 looks like an interesting alternative. 11 ♗d2 exd5 12 ♘d4 is the same position as the game, but with ♗d2 and ...♖d8 included. This needs some testing, but I don't think it'll get any – Lautier's approach is too convincing. That said, any players who need to go for the win should consider this approach.

Black has played 10...0-0-0 in a number of games. Rogozenko suggests 11 ♗d2!? with unclear play – certainly, the black king doesn't feel completely safe on the queenside.

11 ♘d4

By unmasking the d1-h5 diagonal, White hopes to force an exchange on e2, after which he has some chances of generating play on the e-file. 11 ♛xd5?! ♛xd5 12 ♘xd5 0-0-0 is better for Black, if anything.

11...♘xd4!

Lautier's simple approach could be Black's best. Instead, 11...♗xe2 12 ♛xe2+ ♗e7 leaves White with definite compensation. Kobaliya-Ghaem Maghami, Stepanakert 2004 is a typical example: 13 ♘xc6 bxc6 14 0-0 ♔f8 15 ♗d2 ♘f6 16 ♖fe1 ♛d8 17 ♖ac1 and Rogozenko's verdict is accurate: "White has very good compensation for the pawn. In principle the question is only if Black will succeed to escape [sic] after returning material, since otherwise it is difficult to complete development."

12 ♗xh5 (D)

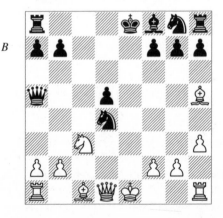

B

Black now has an important decision to make.

12...♘c6

Rowson gives 12...♘e6 as an interesting alternative.

12...♗c5?! is dubious: 13 ♗e3 ♕b4 (if the knight moves, ♕xd5 wins on the spot) 14 ♖c1 ♘f6 15 0-0! ♖d8 16 ♖e1 0-0 17 a3 ♕b3 18 ♗xd4 ♕xd1 19 ♖cxd1 ♗xd4 20 ♖xd4 ♘xh5 21 ♘xd5 and the huge disparity in the two sides' piece placement means that Black will have an uphill struggle.

13 0-0

Analysis by Rowson suggests that Black can equalize after 13 ♕xd5 ♕xd5 14 ♘xd5 by 14...♖d8 (castling queenside is impossible since the king must defend the f7-pawn) 15 ♘c7+ ♔d7 16 ♘d5 g6 17 ♗d1!? (getting out of the reach of the black knight) 17...♔c8 18 ♘c3 (18 ♗b3 ♘d4 is good for Black) 18...♖e8+ 19 ♔f1 f5 20 ♗f4 ♗h6 21 ♗xh6 ♘xh6 22 ♗f3 ♘f7, when Black controls enough central squares to hold the balance – White will have a tough time hanging on to his f3-bishop.

13...♘f6 14 ♗g5 ♗e7 *(D)*

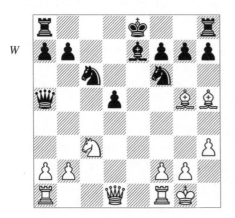

White has several active pieces, but they aren't coordinating too well. In particular, it's hard to see why the bishop is on h5 – put it on b5 and White has a winning position.

15 ♗xf6

Bailing out. 15 ♖e1 0-0 leaves White struggling to show any real compensation.

15...♗xf6 16 ♘xd5 ♗e5!

White's initiative has completely evaporated. Lautier's calm move keeps the e-file closed and prepares to castle. I'd be squeamish about playing this position over the board without home analysis, but Lautier is renowned for his excellent preparation and had obviously solved all the problems at home.

17 ♕b3

Now Black is able to demonstrate clear-cut equality. 17 b4!? is an interesting way to keep the game alive, but I think that after 17...♕d8 18 ♖e1 0-0 19 b5 ♗xa1 20 bxc6 ♗f6 21 cxb7 ♖b8 the game is dynamically balanced.

17...0-0!

A well-calculated finish.

18 ♕xb7 ♕xd5 19 ♗f3 ♕d4 20 ♕xc6 ♖ac8!

This equalizes on the spot, though 20...♕xb2 is fine too.

21 ♕d5 ♕xd5 22 ♗xd5 ♗xb2 ½-½

A neat game by Lautier, which could spell the end of 10 d5 as a winning attempt.

Conclusions

1) 5...♗g4 looks like an excellent equalizing line. White seems to have some menacing options, but they all have been defused.

2) If White doesn't try 10 d5, I don't think Black has any problems. That said, after 10 d5, I find Lautier's approach very convincing. This is a line where White seriously needs an improvement. The only drawback from Black's point of view is that he must be satisfied with a draw since the position becomes so symmetrical and simplified.

Game 20
Mohamad Al Sayed – Ahmed Adly
Arab Ch, Dubai 2005

1 e4 c5 2 c3 d5 3 exd5 ♕xd5 4 d4 *(D)*
4...♘c6

4...cxd4 5 cxd4 e5 is the accelerated version of the line we see in our featured game. White is

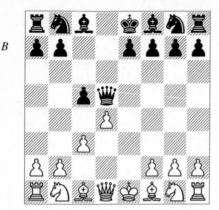

well advised to offer a transposition with 6 ♘f3 (and 6...♘c6 is best in response), since 6 dxe5?! ♕xd1+! 7 ♔xd1 ♘c6 8 f4 ♗f5 followed by 9...0-0-0 gives Black enormous compensation.

5 ♘f3 cxd4

I suppose this is the kind of move some players would choose without thinking, but in fact it profoundly changes the nature of the position. Black weakens the d-pawn and eliminates White's dxc5 option – both of these are big pluses. But there's also a substantial minus – by removing the pawn from the c3-square (in effect, he's taking the c3- and c5-pawns off the board) he allows White to play ♘c3, hitting the black queen. If this queen were to retreat, in addition to the loss of time, Black would have to worry about White advancing with d5, gaining further time and space. Accordingly, this simple move puts Black into a critical position, and he has to play very accurately to justify his play.

6 cxd4 e5!?

This line was popularized by GM Joe Gallagher in *Beating the Anti-Sicilians*. It's a fairly risky line, which needs some good preparation from Black.

6...♗g4 is rarely played, since after 7 ♘c3! White appears to have an advantage. 7...♕h5 is met by 8 ♗e2, and if 7...♗xf3 8 ♘xd5 (8 gxf3 ♕xd4 9 ♕xd4 ♘xd4 10 ♘b5 is far from clear) 8...♗xd1 9 ♘c7+ ♔d7 10 ♘xa8 ♗h5 11 d5 ♘b4 12 ♗f4 White's knight can't be trapped.

7 ♘c3

After any other continuation, Black is doing extremely well. White has to try to exploit the combination of Black's early queen development and opening of the position.

7...♗b4 (D)

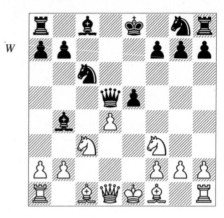

Moving the queen isn't an option.

8 ♗d2

8 dxe5 ♕xd1+ 9 ♔xd1 ♗g4 is very pleasant for Black.

8...♗xc3

Pretty much forced, but now Black must be very careful about his dark squares.

9 ♗xc3

The bishop may look like a big pawn at the moment, but once the d-pawn starts moving, the pressure down the a1-h8 diagonal will be a major source of worry for Black.

9...e4 (D)

Trying the keep the centre relatively closed. Remarkably, Black is the one with the space advantage, at least for the moment. White now has a choice between two very different and roughly equivalent continuations.

9...exd4 is completely wrong, leaving the c3-bishop breathing fire after 10 ♘xd4 ♘ge7 11 ♘xc6 ♕xc6, though capturing on g7 immediately is double-edged: 12 ♗xg7 ♖g8 13 ♗c3 ♗h3!.

10 ♘e5

This is the 'positional line'. One good thing about the move is that it blocks the black queen's path to the kingside, which means that White can develop his f1-bishop in relative comfort.

10 ♘d2 is much sharper. After 10...♘f6 11 ♗c4 ♕g5 12 d5 ♘e5 13 ♗b5+ ♗d7 14 ♗xd7+

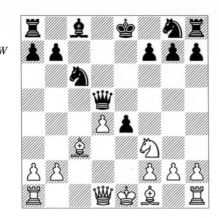

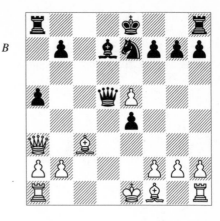

♘exd7 15 0-0 0-0 16 d6 it seems that the advanced d-pawn is more of a strength than a weakness, plus the c3-bishop is dominant. That said, Fritz likes Black here, and so do some GMs.

10...♘xe5

Otherwise 11 ♗c4 would create enormous problems for the f7-pawn.

11 dxe5 ♘e7!

Exchanging on d1 is far too compliant – you don't just bring your opponent's rook into play for no reason.

12 ♕a4+

It's not clear what else White can play. 12 ♗e2 0-0 leaves Black with no problems at all.

12...♗d7 13 ♕b4!?

By hitting the knight, White hopes to make castling difficult for his opponent. 13 ♕a3 ♕e6 looks level; for instance, 14 ♕b4 ♗c6 15 ♗b5 ♖c8 16 0-0 ♘d5 17 ♗xc6+ ♕xc6 18 ♕xe4 ♘xc3 19 ♕xc6+ ♖xc6 20 bxc3 ♖xc3 and a draw is extremely likely.

13...a5 14 ♕a3 *(D)*

This position is typical of the whole c3 Sicilian – Black has minor coordination difficulties which, while theoretically soluble, are still unpleasant to deal with, especially without theoretical preparation.

14...♗c6 15 ♖d1 ♕e6 16 ♕c5!

Covering the c4-square.

16...♖c8

16...♕xa2? loses in spectacular fashion: 17 ♗c4 ♕a4 18 ♗xf7+!? ♔xf7 19 e6+ with a winning attack.

17 ♗c4

Developing with gain of time.

17...♕g4

17...♕g6 is similar.

18 0-0 0-0 *(D)*

Black has a trick which regains the piece.

18...e3 19 f3 is good for White, because 19...♗xf3?? loses to 20 ♕b5+.

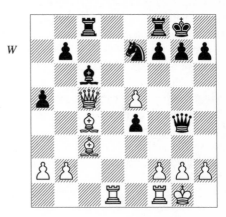

19 ♕xe7 e3 20 f3 ♕xc4 21 ♖d4!?

21 ♖fe1 is also good for White.

21...♕e2

After this compliant move, White's advantage is not in doubt. However, 21...♕xa2 22 ♕g5! f6 23 exf6 ♖xf6 24 ♕xe3 also looks very good for White – the black king is exposed, and opposite-coloured bishops favour the attacker.

22 ♕h4 ♗b5 23 ♖e1 ♕f2+

23...♕c2 24 ♖xe3 ♕b1+ 25 ♖e1 ♕xa2 26 e6! blasts open the black kingside – after 26...fxe6 27 ♕g5 the twin threats of ♕xb5 and ♖d7 compel Black to sacrifice the exchange on c3, but he doesn't get nearly enough compensation.

24 ♕xf2+ exf2+ 25 ♔xf2 a4 26 a3 ♗c4?!

26...♖fd8 27 ♖b4 ♖d5 is more tenacious.

27 ♖ed1 *(D)*

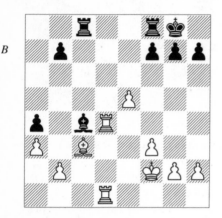

With total domination of the d-file, White has excellent winning chances. Black can't exchange one pair of rooks, let alone the two pairs he needs to draw, and so cannot meet White's simple plan of advancing his kingside majority.

27...b5 28 g4 h6 29 f4 ♖fe8 30 ♖1d2 ♔h7 31 f5

There's nothing Black can do to stop the advance of the white pawns.

31...g6

Not 31...♖xe5 32 ♖xc4.

32 ♖d7 gxf5 33 gxf5 *(D)*

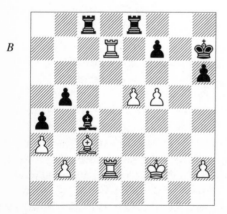

Such a pawn-formation offers White three excellent plans:

1) Creating a passed pawn with e6;

2) Playing f6 in some circumstances;

3) In the interim, using the pawns to control key squares on the sixth rank.

These ideas, coupled with the continued exposure of the black king, explain Black's decision to sacrifice the exchange. However, the resulting position poses very few technical problems to White.

33...♖c5 34 ♔e3 ♖exe5+ 35 ♗xe5 ♖xe5+ 36 ♔f4 ♖c5 37 ♖c2 ♖c6 38 ♖g2 ♗a2 39 ♖d8 ♖c4+ 40 ♔e3 ♖c6 41 ♖gg8! f6 *(D)*

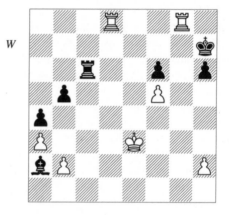

42 ♖g1!

Now the seventh rank is fatally weak.

42...♖c5 43 ♖d7+ ♔h8 44 ♔f4 ♖c4+ 45 ♔g3 ♖c5 46 ♔g4 ♗g8 47 h4 ♗h7 48 ♖d8+ ♔g7 1-0

White wins the bishop with 49 ♔h5+ ♔f7 50 ♖d7+.

Conclusions

1) 5...cxd4 is an extremely sharp move which can't be played without good preparation. I think 6...♗g4 is dubious, but the line with 6...e5 is holding up OK.

2) On move 10, White has a major choice to make. If the 6...e5 line is to be refuted, I have a feeling that 10 ♘d2 is the move to do it. The resulting positions are very double-edged but seem to give White good chances.

3) 10 ♘e5 leads to a dour positional struggle. Black must be quite close to equality but, as our main game illustrates, even these quiet positions contain some poison.

Game 21
Dražen Sermek – Miso Cebalo
Croatian Team Ch, Šibenik 2005

1 e4 c5 2 c3 d5 3 exd5 ♕xd5 4 d4 g6 *(D)*

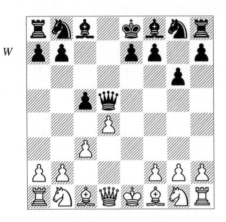

This is one of Black's more interesting options.

5 ♘f3

The immediate 5 ♘a3 cxd4 6 ♘b5 is an alternative with a lot of bark and little bite. After 6...♘a6 7 ♕xd4 (7 ♗e3 ♗g7 8 ♗xd4 ♗xd4 9 ♕xd4 ♕xd4 10 ♘xd4 is the same endgame but without dark-squared bishops – Black must be fine here) 7...♕xd4 8 ♘xd4 it's hard to believe that Black will have any problems holding the endgame, though there may be scope for investigation – after Kurajica's 8...e5 (8...♘f6 is more sedate), for instance, 9 ♘b5 ♘f6 10 ♘f3 e4 11 ♗g5!? seems to give White good chances.

If Black is uneasy about the 5 ♘a3 systems, he should use the move-order 4...♘f6 5 ♘f3 g6, which cuts out this possibility.

5...♗g7 6 ♘a3 *(D)*

Again we see the development of a knight to the rim, with ideas of ♘b5 or ♗c4.

6 c4 is a lesser-known option which is recommended by Rozentalis and Harley. We've yet to see a good GM take the black pieces, and certainly 6...♕d8 7 d5 ♘f6 8 ♘c3 0-0 9 ♗e2 e6 10 0-0 exd5 11 cxd5 looked like an edge in Rozentalis-Piesina, Vilnius 2002, but after 6...♕d6 Black has better chances of equalizing.

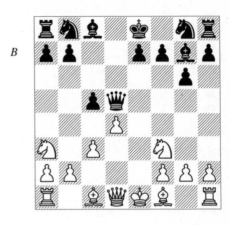

6...♘f6

This is not the only move at Black's disposal. 6...cxd4 is a tricky move-order, in which White must be well-prepared or tactically alert. 7 ♗c4! ♕e4+ 8 ♗e3! leads to similar positions to the main line – Black can't play 8...dxe3?? in view of 9 ♗xf7+! ♔f8 10 ♕d8+ ♔xf7 11 ♘g5+.

7 ♗c4

One of the main points behind White's 6th move was the preparation of this bishop development. Instead, 7 ♘b5 ♘a6 looks comfortable for Black.

7...♕e4+

Other moves look too passive.

8 ♗e3

White is now threatening ♗xf7+, so it's a good idea to castle.

8...0-0 9 0-0 *(D)*

9 dxc5 ♘g4 is fine for Black.

9...cxd4

Dealing with the threat to the c5-pawn.

At first, I thought I'd recommend 9...♗g4 since the endgame after 10 dxc5 ♗xf3 11 ♕xf3 ♕xf3 12 gxf3 isn't completely clear, despite White's extra pawn and two bishops. After some natural moves, such as 12...♖c8 13 ♖fe1 ♔f8 14 ♖ad1 ♘bd7 15 b4 a5, the counterplay looks substantial. However, it seems that White retains a substantial advantage with 16 ♗c1!;

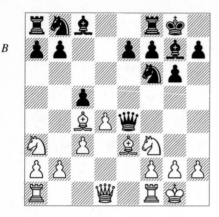

B

for instance, 16...axb4 17 cxb4 b6 18 ♗b5 bxc5 19 ♗xd7 ♘xd7 20 ♖xd7 cxb4 21 ♘b5 ♖xa2 22 ♔g2 with excellent winning chances. That said, I wouldn't be surprised if someone finds an acceptable way to play the endgame after move 12.

10 ♘xd4

This is clearly White's best in my opinion.

10 ♗xd4 has also been extensively tested. The idea can be seen after 10...♘c6 11 ♖e1 ♕f5 12 ♗e5!, when taking on e5 costs material. On the other hand, Black has reasonable development and no weaknesses, so I think he can equalize here. Glek's plan of ...♕h5, ...a6, ...b5, ...♖d8 and ...♗b7 is probably the most reliable.

10...♕e5

Giving the queen more retreat options, while incidentally threatening ...♘g4.

10...♘c6 11 ♖e1 pushes the queen towards the kingside, and away from the forthcoming weakness. 11...♕h4 12 ♘xc6 bxc6 *(D)* is another common position in this line.

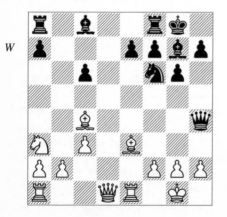

W

In Pavasović-Zarnicki, Pinamar 2002, Black equalized after 13 ♕a4 ♗e6!, but White improved in Pavasović-Movsesian, Croatian Team Ch, Rabac 2003 by 13 ♕f3! ♘g4 (this threat to h2 doesn't pose many problems, but White has an edge in all lines) 14 ♗f4 ♕f6 15 ♖ad1 h5. Now the innovative 16 ♗c7! was strong: 16...♗f5 (after 16...♕xf3 17 gxf3 White wins the e7-pawn – compromising the white kingside is a minor price to pay, since Black has no real way to attack these pawns and White retains a healthy queenside majority) 17 h3 ♘h6 18 ♕e3 ♖fe8 19 ♗f4! and the threat of 20 ♗g5 was decisive.

11 ♕f3

This is a perfect square for the queen and a neat way to prevent the ...♘g4 idea.

11...♘c6!

Eliminating the strong d4-knight at the cost of some structural loosening. 11...♘g4 doesn't achieve anything after 12 ♗f4. It seems difficult to avoid any weaknesses; for instance, 11...♘bd7 12 ♖fe1 ♕b8 13 ♗f4 e5 14 ♗g3 left Black under pressure in Sermek-Feletar, Pula 2001.

12 ♘xc6

White might as well take, since otherwise Black makes a favourable exchange without incurring any weaknesses.

12...bxc6 *(D)*

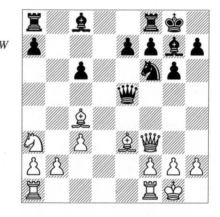

W

13 ♖fe1

This move is automatic – apart from the threat to the black queen, the e7-pawn will now be under surveillance. This pawn is a constant source of concern in fianchetto structures, since it lacks piece protection and can't advance without significantly weakening the dark squares.

White should definitely avoid 13 ♕xc6? ♞g4 14 g3 ♖b8, when Black has an enormous initiative.

13...♕c7

The queen is better placed here than on h4 (see the note to Black's 10th move).

14 ♗f4

Perhaps 14 ♗d4 is a slight improvement, since 14...♞g4 15 ♕g3 ♕xg3 16 hxg3 ♗xd4 17 cxd4 e6 18 ♗e2! ♞f6 19 ♗f3 is a little better for White in view of his superb bishop.

14...♕b7

The queen is excellently placed on b7, since it monitors both c6 and e7 while attacking b2.

15 ♗b3

15 ♕e2 ♗f5! doesn't give White much either.

15...a5! *(D)*

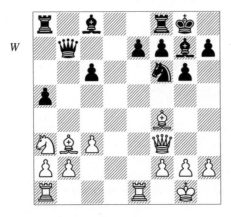

A standard way to play against the b2-pawn. This is one of those positions which looks much better for White, but Black's counterplay proves fully sufficient.

16 ♗a4

Creatively stopping ...a4 while putting pressure on c6.

16...♖a6 17 ♞c4 ♗e6 18 ♕d3

18 b3 is the alternative defence, but ask the a4-bishop what it thinks about this move.

18...♗xc4!?

A non-standard way to proceed, but Cebalo obviously has faith in the knight, which is about to occupy d5.

19 ♕xc4 ♞d5 20 ♗g3 e6 21 ♗d6

This bishop manoeuvre doesn't help. 21 ♖ad1 is a better shot at an edge.

21...♖c8 22 ♗c5 ♖aa8 23 ♖e2 ♖d8 24 ♖d1 *(D)*

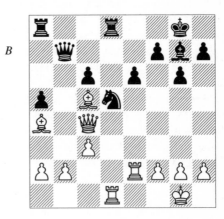

Now all the preparations have been completed for ...♞b6, so:

24...♞b6!

Equalizing.

25 ♖xd8+ ♖xd8 26 ♗xb6 ♕xb6 27 g3 ½-½

White's advantage (if any) is nominal.

Conclusions

1) 4...g6 is a very playable way to meet the c3 Sicilian. Black's bishop is well placed on the long diagonal.

2) Early ♞b5 ideas demand some care on Black's part, but I don't think they are the best way to handle the position.

3) In the main line, as examined, White retains a pleasant advantage due to his central control. This is often converted into a structural advantage, as in the game.

7 Second-Move Alternatives for Black

1 e4 c5 2 c3

Black's main defences in the c3 Sicilian prevent the two-abreast pawn-centre, either through forcing the e-pawn to advance (2...♘f6) or eliminating the e-pawn (2...d5).

The systems in this chapter are a little different. They either prevent a two-abreast pawn-centre through a third-move hit (2...e6 3 d4 d5), a pin (2...♛a5) or extra control of d4 (2...e5), or allow the two-abreast pawn-centre with the aim of generating pressure against it. With most of these lines, I think White has excellent chances of retaining an edge if he knows what he's doing, but 2...g6 is proving a tough nut to crack. We examine these lines as follows:

2...g6 is one of Black's best options. Game 22, Pavasović-del Rio, features a rare reversal for one of the c3 Sicilian's stalwarts.

2...d6 is a method of preparing ...♘f6 by stopping e5, but allows White to get a perfect centre. See Game 23, Goloshchapov-Nevednichy, for the details.

2...e6 is a tacit invitation to a French, but White can keep the game within c3 Sicilian channels, as he does in Game 24, Tiviakov-Berkes.

2...b6 and some lesser options are featured in Game 25, Erenburg-Postny.

Game 22
Duško Pavasović – Salvador del Rio Angelis
European Ch, Warsaw 2005

1 e4 c5 2 c3 g6 *(D)*

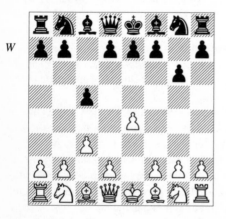

W

This is an interesting sideline which has been used by several strong players. When I audaciously chose the 2 c3 Sicilian, as White, against Sveshnikov at the Calvia Olympiad 2004, it was

this variation he selected. Such a combination of objective strength and relative obscurity is rarely found in openings these days, and I consider this line a really excellent choice for Black – he gets good chances in a dynamic position. By the time most c3 Sicilian players have worked through the theory of 2...♘f6 and 2...d5 most of them will have spent relatively little, if any, time on this move.

3 d4

This is the strongest and most consistent continuation for White. 3 ♘f3 reaches a position which often arises via the 2 ♘f3 g6 3 c3 move-order. Garry Kasparov has played the white side of the position arising after 3...♗g7 4 d4 cxd4 5 cxd4 d5 6 e5 in a couple of blitz games.

3...cxd4

There was a genuine threat to the c5-pawn, so this move is universally played.

Blatny analyses 3...♗g7?! 4 dxc5 ♘a6 5 ♗e3 ♕c7 6 ♘a3! ♘xc5 7 ♘b5 ♕c6 8 ♕d5!, winning material.

4 cxd4 *(D)*

This may seem like a completely automatic move, but it's important to be alert to the possibility of alternatives.

4 ♕xd4 is a valid option, but I think the text-move must be stronger. 4...♘f6 5 e5 (other moves are possible, but promise no advantage) 5...♘c6 6 ♕f4 ♘h5 7 ♕e3 d6 seems to leave Black with his full share of the chances.

Rozentalis and Harley mention the interesting possibility of 4 ♘f3!?, steering towards a Morra Gambit where Black has committed himself to ...g6. Give it a try if you're feeling adventurous.

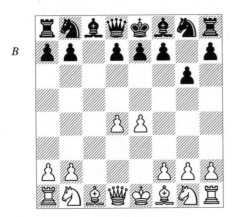

B

4...d5!

This is an important move – other attempts are just too passive. Once White plays ♘c3 and ♘f3, his centre will become impregnable.

That said, 4...♗g7 5 ♘c3 d5 is a line with some surprise value so it's important for White to know what he's doing. The key is to notice that 6 ♘xd5! e6 7 ♘c3 leaves Black with major problems, since 7...♗xd4 8 ♘ge2 ♗xc3+ 9 ♘xc3 ♕xd1+ 10 ♔xd1 gives White a large advantage – two bishops in the endgame, superior development and a slight initiative.

5 ♘c3!?

I chose this against Sveshnikov because it seemed like an attractive and aggressive line, but in fact it has become White's most respected choice here and the selection of both Pavasović

and Sermek. White plays on the tactical features of the position – he offers his e-pawn, at least temporarily, in order to launch a rapid attack against the f7-pawn. There are two alternatives:

a) 5 exd5 ♘f6 transposes into a position from the Caro-Kann once White plays his knight to c3, which he can do immediately or after giving a disruptive check on b5. 6 ♘c3 (6 ♗b5+ ♘bd7 7 ♘c3 ♗g7 8 d6 exd6 9 ♕e2+ ♕e7 10 ♗f4 ♕xe2+ 11 ♗xe2 leaves White with some advantage in a queenless middlegame) 6...♘bd7!? (an interesting choice by the Australian GM) 7 ♗g5 ♗g7 8 ♗e2 ♘b6 9 ♗xf6 ♗xf6 10 ♗f3 0-0 11 ♘ge2 ♗g7 was played in Collins-I.Rogers, British League (4NCL) 2003/4, and here I should have chosen 12 ♕b3 with a normal opening advantage.

b) 5 e5 ♘c6 6 ♘c3 ♗g7 7 ♗b5 gives White some advantage in view of his extra central space. Black, for his part, should aim for the ...f6 break.

5...dxe4 6 ♗c4 *(D)*

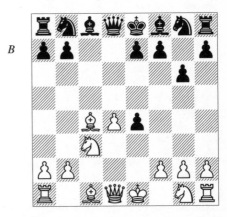

B

This is the point – White is going to launch a rapid attack on the f7-square, compelling Black to play ...e6, which, in combination with ...g6, weakens his dark squares.

6...♘f6

The inattentive 6...♗g7?! 7 ♕b3 e6 8 d5 is good for White.

7 ♕b3 e6 8 d5

Playing to break the black structure.

8...♕b6!?

This novelty could be a big move. Black takes on structural weaknesses in order to exchange queens and seize the initiative. In particular, his control over the d3-square might be a big asset. 8...exd5 9 ♘xd5 ♘xd5 10 ♗xd5 ♕e7! 11 ♕c3 ♕b4 is meant to lead to an equal endgame. After 12 ♗d2 ♕xc3 13 ♗xc3 ♖g8, in my game against Sveshnikov, I got into major trouble after 14 ♘h3? (prompting Alex Baburin and Irish team captain Eamon Keogh to spend *a full week* repeatedly setting up this position and asking novices, passers-by and infants what they'd play with White – each of their selections was better than mine), but after 14 ♗xe4 White really doesn't seem to have much.

8...♘a6!? is also worth investigation, aiming for ...♘c5-d3. A sample variation runs 9 ♗b5+ ♗d7 10 dxe6 fxe6 11 ♗e3 (11 ♕xe6+ gives White nothing after 11...♕e7) 11...♘b4!? 12 ♖d1 ♘bd5 and Black has few complaints.

We now return to 8...♕b6 (D):

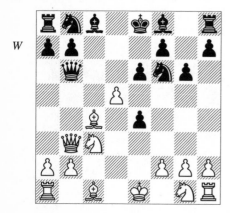

9 ♗b5+

Avoiding the queen exchange with tempo.

9 ♕xb6 axb6 10 dxe6 ♗xe6 11 ♗xe6 fxe6 leaves White with no advantage in the endgame. The poor black structure is amply compensated by piece-play, much as in the game. And of course, he's still a pawn up.

9...♗d7 10 ♗e3

After 10 dxe6 fxe6 it doesn't appear that White has anything better than 11 ♗e3 with a transposition to the game after 11...♗c5.

10...♗c5!

The only move; 10...♕d6 11 dxe6 fxe6 12 ♖d1 is good for White.

11 ♗xc5

I don't think there's anything better. 11 dxe6 fxe6 12 ♗xc5 ♕xc5 13 ♕xe6+ ♕e7 transposes to the game.

11...♕xc5 12 dxe6 fxe6 13 ♕xe6+ ♕e7

Strangely enough, it seems that White has no advantage here.

14 ♕b3?!

This runs into trouble, as we'll see.

Rogozenko suggests 14 ♕c4, threatening ♕c8+. Black's best response is 14...♗xb5 15 ♕xb5+ ♘c6 16 ♘ge2 0-0 17 0-0 with equality.

14 ♕xe7+ ♔xe7 leaves Black with a pleasant endgame; for instance, 15 ♘ge2 ♗xb5 16 ♘xb5 ♘c6 with many aggressive options on the d-file – he can play ...♖hd8 in combination with ...♘b4-d3.

14...a6!

By capturing on d7, White will help Black's development. The position of the queen on b3 is particularly unfortunate in this respect, since Black will be able to gain more time by playing his knight to c5.

15 ♗xd7+ ♘bxd7 (D)

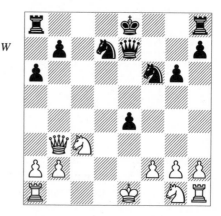

The d3-square is chronically weak.

16 0-0-0

The king doesn't feel particularly safe on the queenside, but there was no real alternative. 16 ♕xb7 ♖b8 17 ♕xa6 ♘c5 18 ♕c6+ ♔f7 leaves White in major trouble – Black has far too many threats, including 19...♘d3+, 19...♖xb2 and 19...♖hd8.

16...♘c5 17 ♕c2 0-0 18 f3

It would be perverse to regard the e4-pawn as a 'weakness' here, so Pavasović plays to liquidate it. The problem is that, in the resulting wide-open position, Black's pieces will be far more active. 18 ♔b1 ♖ac8 19 ♘ge2 is the alternative approach, but White has major problems here too – the e4-pawn is still very strong, and Black has excellent play down the c- and f-files.

18...♖ac8 19 ♔b1 b5

Now White is getting hit everywhere.

20 ♘h3

Of course, 20 fxe4?! ♘cxe4 is even worse for White.

20...exf3!

This is the right time to make this capture, since the knight can no longer take back.

21 gxf3 (D)

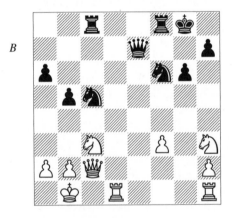

Now White has an inferior structure as well as poorly-placed pieces.

21...♕e3 22 ♕g2 ♘d3

22...♖fd8! gives some genuine attacking chances, and might be a better shot.

23 ♕d2

23 ♕e2 is a tighter defence, but White still has an inferior endgame.

23...♕xd2 24 ♖xd2 ♘e5

The endgames are just as good as the middlegames for Black.

25 f4 ♘c4 26 ♖d4 ♖fe8 27 f5

Sacrificing a pawn for a little activity (now it's Black who will have the weak pawn on the f-file). This is a reasonable practical shot but, objectively, must leave Black with excellent winning chances. Perhaps there was also an element of shellshock – Pavasović isn't used to

defending horrible endgames in his pet opening.

27...gxf5 28 ♖g1+ ♔f8! 29 ♘f4 ♔f7!

Having side-stepped ♘g5+, Black puts his king on a better square.

30 b3 ♘e5 31 ♖g3 ♘g6 32 ♘cd5 ♘xd5 33 ♖xd5 ♖e1+ 34 ♔b2 ♘e7

Black could also have fallen into the 'trap': 34...♘xf4 35 ♖xf5+ ♔e6 36 ♖xf4 ♖e2+ 37 ♔a3 ♖xh2 with a promising position.

35 ♖d7 ♖c6 (D)

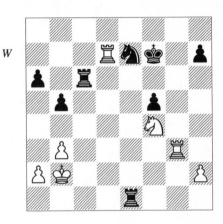

36 ♖a7

Playing for the rook and pawn endgame with 36 ♘d5 isn't so hot. Apart from the fact that such endgames would give Black superb winning chances since the white king is cut off, it seems that White can't even achieve one of these dismal positions since 36...♖e2+ 37 ♔b1 (37 ♔a3 ♖cc2) 37...♖h6 is extremely strong.

36...b4 37 a3 ♖ec1

Threatening mate.

38 ♖g2 bxa3+ 39 ♔xa3 ♖c7!

A cute method to simplify the position.

40 ♖xa6 ♖a1+ 41 ♖a2 ♖xa2+ 42 ♔xa2 ♖c2+ 43 ♔b1 ♖xh2 44 b4 ♖h4 45 ♘d3 ♘d5 46 ♖a7+ ♔f6 47 ♔c2 ♘xb4+ 48 ♘xb4 ♖xb4 49 ♖xh7 ♖d4!

Cutting off the king.

50 ♖h1 ♖d7 51 ♖f1 ♔g5 52 ♖g1+ ♔h4 53 ♖f1 ♔g4 54 ♖g1+ ♔h3 55 ♖f1 ♖d5!

Now that the pawn is defended, the king can advance.

56 ♔c3 ♔g2 57 ♔c4 ♖e5 58 ♖b1 f4

The position is now a simple win.

59 ♔d3 ♖e7 60 ♖b2+ ♔g3 61 ♖b8 f3 62 ♖g8+ ♔f2 63 ♔d2 ♖d7+ 64 ♔c2 ♔e2 65 ♖e8+ ♔f1 66 ♖f8 f2 67 ♖f6 ♔g2 0-1

Maybe White lost on time here, since the text-move isn't the way to win this endgame ('building a bridge' with 67...♖d5! is standard).

This was an excellent win for del Rio – it's a rare event when Pavasović gets out-prepared in a c3 Sicilian.

Conclusions

1) 2...g6 is one of Black's best ways of countering the c3 Sicilian. A lot of tension is maintained, and there is no way for White to force a draw while staying in theory (as he can do in one or two of the other lines).

2) On move 5, White has three major options. I think this game is further evidence against 5 ♘c3, so he should go for one of the other attempts. I'd pick 5 e5. Have a look at Game 8, Baklan-Romero, for some tips on how to handle these positions.

3) 8...♕b6 is just an excellent move. If you learn the lines in this game well, your next game as Black in the c3 Sicilian could be a very pleasant experience.

Game 23

Alexander Goloshchapov – Vladislav Nevednichy
Miskolc 2004

1 e4 c5 2 c3 d6

This variation has no real, established main line. Instead, there is a collection of six or seven key positions.

3 d4 ♘f6 *(D)*

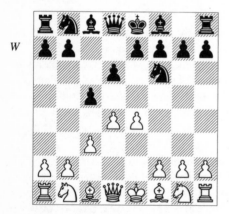

Threatening the e4-pawn. White has a few options here.

4 ♗d3

4 f3 is also a good move.

4 dxc5 ♘c6! is OK for Black – 5 ♗d3 transposes to the game and 5 cxd6 ♘xe4 6 ♗e3 (6 dxe7? ♕xd1+ 7 ♔xd1 ♘xf2+ 8 ♔e1 ♘xh1 9 exf8♕+ ♔xf8 10 g3 ♗f5 is winning for Black) 6...♘xd6 leaves White with no advantage.

4...♘c6

4...cxd4 5 cxd4 g6 is the main alternative. Collins-A.Hunt, Blackpool 2003 continued 6 ♘c3 ♗g7 7 h3 0-0 8 ♘f3 ♘c6 9 0-0 e5 10 dxe5 dxe5 11 ♗e3 ♖e8 12 ♗b5 ♗d7 13 ♕b3 ♘a5 14 ♕a4 with the more pleasant game for White (since his pieces are more active), though Black had few problems holding the position.

The immediate 4...g6 runs into 5 dxc5! dxc5 6 e5 ♘d5 (6...c4? just loses a pawn to 7 ♕a4+ and 8 ♕xc4) 7 ♗e4 ♘c7 8 ♕xd8+ ♔xd8 with a difficult endgame for Black. Tiviakov-Cao Sang, European Ch, Warsaw 2005 is a good illustration of how to handle these positions with White: 9 ♗e3 (Tiviakov suggests 9 ♘a3 and 9 f4 as promising alternatives) 9...♘d7 10 f4 f6 11 ♘d2 ♗h6 12 exf6 exf6 13 ♔f2 ♘e6 14 g3 f5 15 ♗g2 ♘f6 16 h3 and Black was struggling.

We now return to 4...♘c6 *(D)*:

5 dxc5

An interesting decision by Goloshchapov – if he was happy with this position, I'm not sure why he didn't play 4 dxc5.

5 ♘f3 attempts to retain the ideal centre. 5...♗g4 6 d5 ♗xf3 (6...♘e5?! 7 ♘xe5 ♗xd1?? loses to 8 ♗b5+) 7 ♕xf3 ♘e5 8 ♗b5+ is a little better for White, since he retains the two bishops and a useful space advantage.

5...d5!?

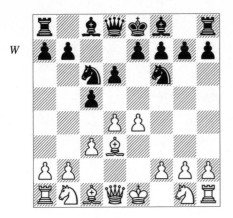

This is an interesting and strong move, but the simple recapture on c5 has never come close to being refuted. For instance, Thipsay-Ravisekhar, Delhi 1982 continued 5...dxc5 6 ♘f3 ♗g4 7 h3 ♗h5 8 g4 ♗g6 9 ♕e2 ♕d7 10 ♘bd2 ♖d8 11 ♗c2 e6 12 0-0 ♗e7 13 ♘c4 ♕c7 14 a4 ♘d7 15 ♘e1 h5 16 f4 hxg4 17 hxg4 f6 18 a5 ♗f7 and, in this unbalanced position with chances for both sides, a draw was agreed.

6 ♘d2 *(D)*

This is the only attempt at advantage. 6 exd5 ♕xd5 is very comfortable for Black – he has superior development and excellent central control, while he is about to recapture the pawn on c5.

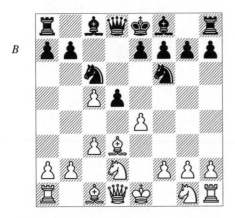

6...e6

This is a little passive – certainly the c8-bishop isn't a fan. 6...e5 is assessed as equal by Rozentalis and Harley. I'm not sure what Nevednichy was scared of in this position.

7 ♘gf3!

Correctly allowing the exchange on e4. 7 ♕e2 is the alternative, but I think Black is comfortable after 7...d4.

7...dxe4?!

I don't think Black should go for this endgame. 7...♗xc5 is more solid. White then has a few tempting options; for instance, 8 exd5 ♘xd5 (8...♕xd5 9 ♕e2 0-0 10 ♘e4 ♗e7 11 ♘xf6+ ♗xf6 12 ♗e4 is also nice for White) 9 ♘e4 ♗e7 10 0-0 0-0 11 ♕e2 ♕c7 12 ♖d1 with an edge.

8 ♘xe4

This natural move is the best; 8 ♗xe4 ♗xc5 is just level.

8...♘xe4 9 ♗xe4 *(D)*

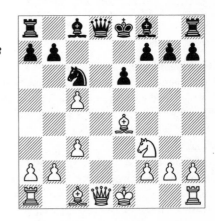

9...♕xd1+

9...♗xc5 leads to an interesting position. If White takes on d8, a similar endgame arises. If he plays 10 ♕e2, I think Black needs to be a little careful. In particular, he should avoid allowing the 'Greek Gift' sacrifice after 10...0-0?!: 11 ♗xh7+!? ♔xh7 12 ♘g5+ ♔g6 (12...♔g8 13 ♕e4 f5 14 ♕h4 ♖f6 15 ♕h7+ ♔f8 16 ♕h8+ ♔e7 17 ♕xg7+ ♔e8 18 ♗f4 with more than enough compensation) 13 h4 f5 (13...♕d5 14 ♕g4 ♗xf2+ 15 ♔xf2 ♕f5+ 16 ♕xf5+ ♔xf5 17 ♔g3 b6 18 ♖f1+ ♔g6 19 ♘xf7! and White wins material) 14 h5+ ♔f6 15 ♘h7+ ♔f7 16 ♘xf8 ♗xf8 17 h6 with a continuing attack.

10 ♔xd1 ♗xc5

It would be easy to look at this endgame and conclude that Black must be fine, but appearances can be deceptive. The problem is that

Black has too many weak squares and pawns to cover (d6, d7, f7 and, in some lines, b7), as shown by the fact that Nevednichy is soon facing serious problems.

11 ♔e2 *(D)*

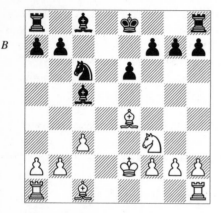

This is the ideal square for the white king in such endgames. It can't be attacked (Black can't get his bishop to the a6-f1 diagonal) and it covers key squares on the d-file as well as protecting the f2-pawn and supporting ♗e3.

11...♗d7

11...e5 looks like a good attempt to mix things up, since Black gets excellent compensation after 12 ♗xc6+?! bxc6 13 ♘xe5 ♗a6+ 14 ♔e1 0-0-0. However, White retains the edge with simple chess: 12 ♖d1 f6 13 b4 with a solid initiative.

12 ♖d1 a5

A typical move, played to restrain the ambitions of White's b-pawn.

13 ♘g5

White now threatens 14 ♘xf7.

13...♘d8 *(D)*

The other defence wouldn't equalize either: 13...♖d8 14 ♗f4 h6 15 ♘f3 and White retains an edge, though I think Black should have gone in for this rather than the game continuation.

14 ♗d3!?

Vacating the e4-square for the knight while preventing ...♗b5+.

14...♗c6 15 ♘e4 ♗e7 16 ♗f4 f6

16...0-0 doesn't help Black, since it just removes his king from the centre.

17 ♘d6+ ♔f8 18 ♗e4

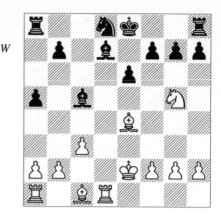

Exchanging light-squared bishops will make b7 and d7 much weaker.

18...e5

This is probably best, even if there's a slight weakening of the d-file. Black prepares to put his knight on a good square.

19 ♗e3 ♗xe4

19...♗xd6 20 ♗xc6 ♘xc6 21 ♖xd6 is horrible for Black – even if his h8-rook were in play, he'd have a hard time containing the white rooks and bishop.

20 ♘xe4 ♘e6 21 ♖d7! *(D)*

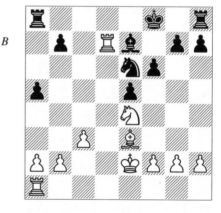

The seizure of the seventh rank is the beginning of the end – a simple comparison of both sides' rooks is enough to establish that Black is lost.

21...f5

The alternative 21...♖b8 22 ♖ad1 is equally horrible for Black.

22 ♘d6 ♗xd6 23 ♖xd6 ♔e7 24 ♖b6 f4?

This is the result of frustration. 24...罝hb8 (so that the a-pawn remains protected) leaves Black with an uphill struggle to hold the position after 25 罝b5 ⚔f6 26 a4, but at least he has his pawns.

25 罝xb7+ ⚔f6 26 ⚌a7!

Not the most conventional square for a bishop, but as well as being untouchable itself, the prelate serves a very useful function in preventing Black from contesting the b-file.

26...罝hd8 27 f3 h5 28 罝d1 罝xd1 29 ⚔xd1 g5 30 ⚌b8!

Cute.

30...a4 31 罝b5 ⚘c5 32 ⚌xe5+ ⚔xe5 33 罝xc5+

Black could have spared himself the rest.

33...⚔f6 34 罝c6+ ⚔f5 35 罝c5+ ⚔f6 36 罝d5 罝b8 37 ⚔c2 罝e8 38 h3 罝e1 39 b4 1-0

Conclusions

1) The 2...d6 system is quite tough for Black to handle. He lets White get a perfect centre, much as in the Pirc Defence.

2) On move 4, White has a few options. My preferences are 4 ⚌d3 and 4 f3.

3) In the main line with 4 ⚌d3, Black needs to watch out for a quick e5. There are a few accurate move-orders he can use to render this idea innocuous. 4...cxd4 is solid, with White retaining a risk-free advantage. 4...⚘c6 is a little more dynamic.

4) The game is a good illustration of how difficult some c3 Sicilian endgames can be for Black, despite their innocuous appearance. Be very careful before you decide exchange the queens.

Game 24

Sergei Tiviakov – Ferenc Berkes

British League (4NCL) 2005/6

1 e4 c5 2 c3 e6 3 d4 d5 *(D)*

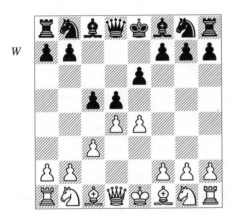

This is an invitation to cross swords in the Advance French after 4 e5. Sveshnikov, whose opening views are as unconventional as they are outspoken, regards 2...e6 as 'a serious mistake' (since the French is, apparently, a dubious opening), but no one else seems to think so. That said, 4 e5 is probably the most ambitious move here – the game continuation is the alternative, and tries to steer the play towards quieter positions which are similar to the Tarrasch French (1 e4 e6 2 d4 d5 3 ⚘d2 and now 3...c5). Indeed, direct transpositions are possible, though not forced.

4 exd5 exd5

There is nothing wrong with 4...⚕xd5, which transposes to 2...d5 3 exd5 ⚕xd5 4 d4 e6.

5 ⚘f3 *(D)*

Now Black can easily go wrong.

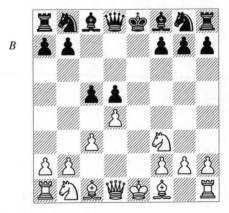

5...⚘c6

These moves represent the most flexible approach, since these knights rarely go to other squares whereas the other pieces have more options (the white bishop can go to e2, d3 or b5, while the g8-knight can develop to either f6 or e7).

5...♘f6 6 ♗g5! creates some unpleasant pressure on d5, since White threatens to capture on f6 and c5. I think Black should avoid this line for this reason.

5...♗d6 has been used by heavyweight GMs Anatoly Karpov and Nigel Short. After 6 ♗b5+ Black has nothing better than transposing to the game with 6...♘c6, since 6...♗d7 7 dxc5! is good for White in view of the threat to the d5-pawn. Other 6th moves don't promise White much – in Garner-Kasparov, Oakham simul 1997, Black gained good play after 6 dxc5 ♗xc5 7 ♗d3 ♘f6 8 0-0 0-0 9 h3 ♘c6 10 ♘bd2 ♗b6 11 ♘b3 ♘e4 12 ♘bd4 ♕f6.

6 ♗b5

The classical approach, known from analogous positions in the Tarrasch French.

6 g3 is a good independent option, aiming to attack the d-pawn by fianchettoing the light-squared bishop.

6...♗d6 (D)

Black loses the 'battle for tempo' by moving his bishop before White played dxc5, but he has to get going with his kingside development.

6...♘f6 7 0-0 ♗e7 8 dxc5 ♗xc5 9 ♖e1+ is dealt with in the note to Black's 8th move.

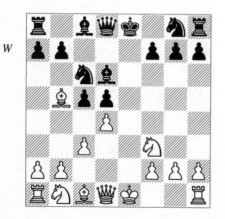

7 dxc5

White has nothing to gain by delaying this move any further.

7...♗xc5 8 0-0

With an open e-file, castling is always the best move. Now ♖e1+ is an idea, while Black is denied any annoying ...♕e7+ possibilities.

8...♘e7

I think this is an inferior square for the knight – it would rather be on f6.

If Black wishes to venture 8...♘f6 though, he needs to be well prepared with some improvements over existing theory, since he has had some problems after both 9 ♘d4 and 9 ♗g5. Note, however, that the immediate attempt to play on the e-file with 9 ♖e1+ ♗e6 10 ♘d4 doesn't work after 10...0-0! because 11 ♘xe6?! fxe6 12 ♖xe6?? loses to 12...♘e4!. This is rather cooperative play by White, but does illustrate how weak his f2-pawn can become.

9 ♘bd2 (D)

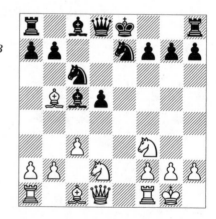

We now have a position which can be reached via Tiviakov's favourite Tarrasch French variation: 1 e4 e6 2 d4 d5 3 ♘d2 c5 4 exd5 exd5 5 ♘gf3 ♘c6 6 ♗b5 ♗d6 7 dxc5 ♗xc5 8 0-0 ♘e7 and now, instead of the universal 9 ♘b3, if White plays 9 c3 we have directly transposed to the game. The move c3 is extremely common in such structures however, and so a direct transposition to the 9 ♘b3 lines will probably occur.

9...a6!?

Berkes kicks the white bishop and prepares a bishop retreat to a7.

9...0-0 is the main continuation, and after 10 ♘b3 Black has a choice of bishop retreats:

a) 10...♗b6 11 ♖e1 ♘f5 12 ♗d3 h6 13 ♗c2 ♗e6 14 ♕d3 ♕f6 15 ♗e3! more or less forces the exchange of dark-squared bishops, with some advantage for White.

b) 10...♗d6 11 ♗d3 h6 12 h3 ♘f5 13 ♖e1 ♕f6 14 ♗c2 ♖d8 15 ♕d3 g6 with complex and balanced play.

10 ♗d3

Not the only move – I think both 10 ♗a4 and 10 ♗e2 have their good points – but I imagine Tiviakov wanted to discourage ...♗f5.

10...♗a7 (D)

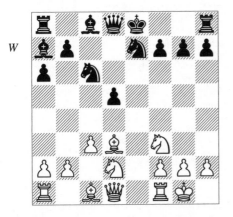

This bishop will have to drop back anyway (in response to ♘b3), so Berkes moves it straight away. On a7 it is quite well placed, since it has the choice of two key diagonals (a7-g1 and b8-h2).

11 ♘b3 ♗g4

Berkes decides to use his bishop actively on the kingside and avoids 11...0-0 12 h3, though this is a rather standard-looking position.

12 ♖e1

This position is most commonly reached via the 1 e4 e6 2 d4 d5 3 ♘d2 a6!? move-order, but with both sides playing one move less! This is yet another example of the universality of IQP positions, where the same positions can be reached via dozens of routes.

12...h6

This is a useful move, cutting out any ♗g5 ideas.

13 ♗e3 (D)

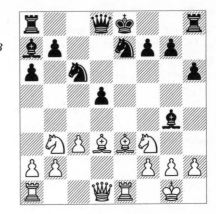

Offering an exchange which is in White's favour – without the dark-squared bishops, White has better chances of establishing control over the d4-square.

13...♗b8!

In several of the preceding games, Black had allowed the dark-squared bishops to be exchanged, which is a mistake. Berkes manages to force an important kingside weakness in the subsequent play by lining up his queen and bishop on the b8-h2 diagonal.

14 ♘bd4

A typical continuation, but White had a promising alternative: Rowson suggests 14 h3 ♗xf3 (14...♗h5 is too loose, since 15 g4! ♗g6 16 ♗xg6 fxg6 17 ♘c5 is good for White) 15 ♕xf3 ♘e5 (15...♕d6 16 g3 ♘e5 17 ♕e2 ♕d7 18 ♗c5! is extremely strong for White) 16 ♕e2 0-0 17 ♖ad1, and this does look like a better shot than the game continuation.

14...0-0 (D)

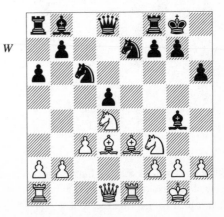

Now White is faced with the difficult task of improving his position. An immediate attack on the d-pawn is out of the question, so he just plays to bring a rook onto the d-file from where it might exert pressure in the long term.

15 ♗e2

On d3, the bishop was only pseudo-active – in fact, it protected the black d-pawn from frontal attacks. Additionally, once the queen's rook comes to d1, White doesn't want his f3-knight to be pinned.

15...♖e8

Always a useful move in these structures. It's interesting that Berkes feels no pressing need to do something constructive with his queen's rook – on a8 it performs a function of sorts, as illustrated by Black's 18th move.

16 ♕a4

Threatening the g4-bishop. It's interesting that Tiviakov refrained from the natural h3, thus gaining a tempo now, though I still agree with Rowson about move 14.

16...♗h5 17 ♖ad1 ♕c7

Black more often arranges to put his queen on d6 and the bishop on c7, but the intention is the same.

18 g3

Otherwise a combination of ...b5, ...♘xd4, ...♗xf3 and ...♕xh2+ could prove embarrassing.

18...♗a7! (D)

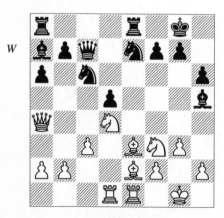

Berkes has played well, and there's no reason to prefer White in this position. The last move, in addition to connecting the rooks, serves the purpose of improving the bishop since its valuable work on the b8-h2 diagonal (forcing a kingside weakness) is complete.

19 ♔g2

Tidying up the kingside.

19...♗g6

I think Berkes has half an eye on the e4-square.

20 ♘xc6

This is an implicit concession that White has nothing – the d-pawn will now be impregnable.

20...bxc6 21 ♗xa7 ♖xa7 (D)

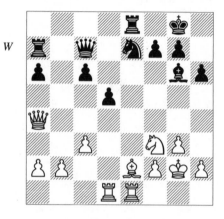

Despite the isolation of the a6-pawn, this structural change is in Black's favour, since the d-pawn is solidly supported. White will never be genuinely able to attack the a-pawn anyway.

22 ♗d3 ♖b8!

The b-file is, in the short term, more important than the e-file.

23 ♗xg6 ♘xg6 24 ♖e2 ♕d7 25 b3 c5!

The weakening of the d-pawn is purely formal.

26 ♕xd7 ♖xd7 27 c4

It's impossible to pressurize the d-pawn when the c-pawn is next to it, since it will always be able to advance.

27 ♖ed2 ♖bd8 28 b4!? is an ambitious attempt to re-isolate Black's d-pawn, but after 28...cxb4 29 cxb4 the fact that this pawn is now passed may have scared Tiviakov off this line. I think he should have gone in for it though.

27...d4 28 ♘e1! (D)

A natural regrouping.

28...a5 29 ♘d3 ♖c7 30 ♘b2

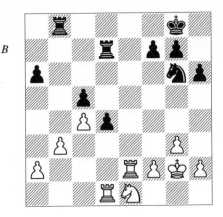

Tiviakov must have been worried about a break with ...a4.

30...♘f8 31 ♖de1 ♘e6 32 f4 g6 33 ♖e5 ♔g7 34 ♔f3 ♔f6 35 ♖d5 ♖bb7 36 ♘a4 ♖c6

The position is balanced. Tiviakov tries advancing the kingside pawns, but it isn't enough.

37 g4 ♖bc7 38 f5 ♘f8 39 ♖e8 ♘d7 40 fxg6 fxg6 41 ♖a8 ♘e5+ 42 ♔g3 ♘d3 43 h4 ♔g7 ½-½

After 44 ♖xa5 ♖e7! Black forces a neat perpetual check on e3, e2 and e1. A precise defence from Berkes.

Conclusions

1) The 2...e6 system is an attempt to steer the game from a c3 Sicilian into an Advance French. How you respond depends on your repertoire. 4 exd5 is the way to keep matters in c3 Sicilian channels.

2) Black often ends up with an IQP in these lines, which means he needs to play accurately in order to avoid falling into a passive position. Study of games in the Tarrasch French, especially those between Karpov and Korchnoi, is very useful for getting ideas on how to play with either colour.

Game 25
Sergei Erenburg – Evgeny Postny
Andorra 2004

1 e4 c5 2 c3 b6

A respectable sideline, used by Israeli GM Artur Kogan (in general, I highly recommend the study of Kogan's games against 1 e4, since he makes excellent scores with sidelines like this and 1 e4 d5 2 exd5 ♕xd5 3 ♘c3 ♕d8!?). I've played it myself, with pretty good results (the only game in my database was a win, but I'm sure that there are a couple of masterpieces from when I was 13).

It's interesting that, after Zviagintsev's 1 e4 c5 2 ♘a3!?, Rowson recommends 2...b6 since the defence of the e-pawn is an awkward one. Here the situation is slightly more favourable for White, since he can get his pawn to d4 and so defend with ♗d3.

We shall take a quick look at a few other moves here too:

a) 2...♘c6 isn't advisable. After 3 d4 cxd4 4 cxd4 d5, White can transpose into Game 20, Al Sayed-Adly, with 5 exd5 ♕xd5 or try either 5 e5 or 5 ♘c3. If Black is happy with the Al Sayed game, he should use the 2...d5 move-order so he doesn't have to worry about these alternatives.

b) 2...♕a5 is a rather exotic method of discouraging d4 (since the c-pawn will be unable to recapture). After 3 ♘f3 ♘c6 4 ♗c4 Black has no clear route to equality. Rozentalis-Miezis, Gausdal 2003 continued 4...♘f6 5 d3 e6 and now 6 ♕e2!, preventing ...d5, would have left White with a stable advantage.

c) 2...e5 is an interesting move which I've used myself in a few games. There is little theory on this move, which has the idea of saving some time compared to the Ruy Lopez (Black frequently needs to move his c6-knight to get his c-pawn to c5 – here, he hopes that he can get a Ruy Lopez with the pawn already on c5). After 3 ♘f3 ♘c6 4 ♗c4 (*D*), White is threatening to generate some quick play against the traditionally vulnerable f7-pawn with ♕b3 or, in some lines, ♘g5.

Then:

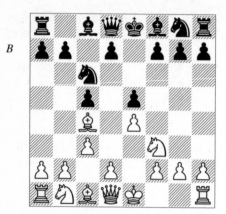

c1) 4...♗e7 allows 5 d4 exd4 6 cxd4 cxd4 7 0-0 with a nice game for White – Black has no way to challenge for control of the centre.

c2) 4...♕c7!? is perhaps the most solid move, since the c6-knight can drop back to d8 and cover the f7-pawn. This isn't such a bad deal for Black, since the white queen would be misplaced on b3 if the f7-pawn didn't fall. 5 0-0 (castling is always the most natural move, but here it has the added benefit of getting a rook on the f-file so that ♘g5 and f4 is an idea; it turns out that Black has no easy way to stop ♘g5 anyway) 5...♗e7 (5...♘f6 6 ♘g5 ♘d8 7 f4 also leaves White with some initiative) 6 ♘g5! ♘d8 (if Black takes by 6...♗xg5, then 7 ♕h5 regains the material) 7 f4! (D).

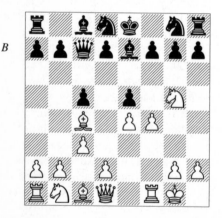

This is the whole point. 7...exf4 8 ♘f3 ♘h6 9 ♕e2 (it's necessary to protect the bishop before playing d4, since otherwise ...cxd4 would threaten ...♕xc4) 9...0-0 10 d4 ♘g4 11 e5 ♘e3

(Black decides at least to 'win the minor exchange', but his pieces are so awful that this doesn't affect the position very much) 12 ♗xe3 fxe3 13 b3! (again, White needs to attend to the defence of the bishop before playing the move he wants to play – 13 ♕xe3? cxd4 is a problem) 13...d6 14 ♕xe3 ♘c6 15 ♕e4 cxd4 16 cxd4 dxe5 17 dxe5 ♗e6 18 ♘c3 ♖ad8 19 ♔h1 ♕b6 20 ♘d5 ♗xd5 21 ♗xd5 and White had the better chances in Sermek-Markowski, Cannes 1997.

We now return to 2...b6 (D):

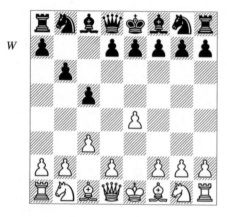

3 d4

Not much to say about this move – White's last move prepared 3 d4 and there's absolutely no reason not to play it now.

3...♗b7

Exchanging on d4 first would be a significant error, since White can then defend the e-pawn with ♘c3. In general, Black only takes on d4 in this line when there is some concrete purpose behind it, such as preparing ...♘b4 to bag the d3-bishop.

4 ♗d3

This is solid and good, but there's a decent alternative. 4 f3 makes a lot of sense, since the b7-bishop is blunted. Play typically continues 4...e6 5 ♗e3 ♘f6 6 ♘d2 (advancing the e-pawn would create an odd impression and liberate Black's light-squared bishop) 6...♘c6 7 a3 ♗e7 8 ♗d3 a5!? (showing another method of exchanging light-squared bishops, even after the queen's knight has been developed) 9 ♘e2 ♗a6 10 ♗xa6 (I don't think it's worth avoiding this exchange, since the bishop is strong on a6 and Black has some tender dark squares on the queenside) 10...♖xa6 11 0-0 0-0 12 ♘f4 was played in Rozentalis-Tyomkin, Montreal 2000. I think White's position is clearly preferable, since Black has no counterplay.

We now return to the position after 4 ♗d3 *(D)*:

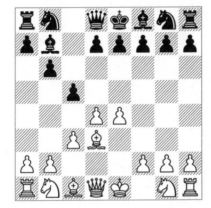

B

4...g6!?

This is a relatively new approach. Black adopts a double fianchetto formation in a relatively favourable form, since White has trouble aggressively developing his queen's knight. The black position requires a lot of subtlety to handle though, so for less experienced players I'd recommend something more conventional (see the rest of the book!).

4...♘f6 is a more established continuation, but that doesn't count for much in such a line – players are often just making it up as they go along. Then:

a) 5 e5? might be a good idea if Black had to reply 5...♘d5 6 c4 ♘b4 7 d5, etc., but he has 5...♗xg2 at his disposal.

b) 5 d5 runs into 5...c4!, deflecting the white bishop from its defence of the e-pawn. The game Bojković-Kogan, Nova Gorica 1997 continued 6 ♗xc4 ♘xe4 7 ♕d3 (a natural attempt to dislodge the knight from its strong central square) 7...♘d6! *(D)*.

The knight is well placed here; the one concern is the development of the remaining horse, but Kogan has an innovative plan in mind. 8 ♗b3 ♘a6 (White can't cover the c5-square, and

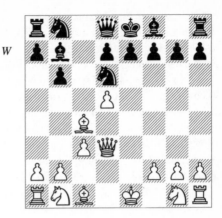

W

I already prefer the black position) 9 c4 (solidifying the d5-pawn and thus playing against the b7-bishop) 9...b5!? (Black had more sedate alternatives like 9...♘c5 and 9...e6, but Kogan's move cracks open the white structure; there's also a big psychological benefit to playing a move your opponent has been trying to stop, and White's last move was clearly directed, in part, against ...b5) 10 cxb5 (White has nothing better) 10...♘c5 11 ♕d1 ♕a5+ 12 ♘c3 ♘xb5 13 ♘ge2 ♘xc3 14 ♘xc3 ♗a6 15 ♗c2 e5 and Black was doing fine.

c) 5 ♕e2 aims to put the queen's knight on c3 rather than d2. After 5...cxd4 6 cxd4 ♘c6 7 ♘f3 ♘b4 8 ♘c3 ♘xd3+ 9 ♕xd3, Artur Kogan developed the move 9...♕c8!, aiming to play ...♗a6. 10 ♗g5 *(D)* is clearly the most dangerous reply, bringing the last minor piece into play with immediate pressure on the f6-knight.

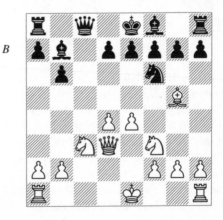

B

Then:

c1) 10...♗a6 ran into trouble in Keitling-haus-Kogan, Lazne Bohdanec 1996: 11 ♕e3 e6 12 0-0-0 (White could put a rook on the c-file instead, but he's aiming for a central knockout) 12...♘g4 13 ♕f4!? ♗b4 (13...♘xf2 can be met by 14 ♘e5 f6 15 ♕xf2, with excellent chances for White) 14 ♕xg4 ♗xc3 15 ♔b1! (taking the bishop is out of the question) 15...♗b4 16 ♘e5! (the pieces can't be forked by ...f6 in view of ♕h5+) 16...♕b7 17 d5 (opening the d-file and weakening the d7-e6-f7 cluster) 17...h5 18 ♕g3 ♖c8 19 a3 ♗c5 20 ♖he1 (White's central dominance is overwhelming) 20...♗b5 21 ♗h4 ♗f8 22 d6 ♖h6 23 ♗g5 ♖h7 24 ♕f4 g6 25 ♕f6 ♕b8 (White has improved his position as much as possible, so now it's time for the sacrifice) 26 ♘xg6! ♗xd6 (26...fxg6 loses to 27 ♕xg6+ and ♖e3!) 27 ♗f4 ♗e7 28 ♕xe7# (1-0).

c2) 10...d5 11 ♗xf6 dxe4 12 ♘xe4 gxf6 13 0-0 ♗h6 (D) leads to a position that is quite tricky to assess, since the looseness of Black's position is well compensated by his two bishops.

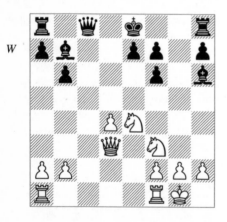

In Vlasov-Kogan, Moscow 2002, White tried an interesting pawn sacrifice: 14 ♘g3 e6 15 d5!? (enticing the bishop to the d5-square so ♘f5 can be played) 15...♗xd5 16 ♘f5 ♗f8 17 ♖fd1 ♕b7 18 ♖ac1 a6 (Black's salvation lies in the fact that White has no pawn-breaks against the e6-f6-f7 cluster) 19 ♘3h4 ♖g8 20 g3 ♖g5 21 ♕d4 ♗e4 22 ♘d6+ ♗xd6 23 ♕xd6 ♖d5 24 ♖xd5 ♕xd5 25 ♕xb6 ♕d2 26 ♖f1 and an interesting game had dissolved into approximate equality.

d) 5 ♘d2 cxd4 (once the white knight has committed itself to d2, Black should make this capture) 6 cxd4 ♘c6 (D) and now:

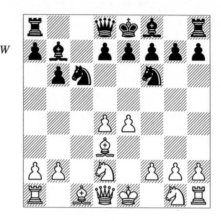

d1) 7 ♕a4!? is an interesting option: 7...e6 8 a3 ♗e7 9 ♘e2 0-0 10 0-0 d6 11 b4 a6 12 ♗b2 with a stable space advantage for White, Smagin-I.Sokolov, Novi Sad 1986.

d2) After 7 ♘e2 White has, in general, been demonstrating a pleasant advantage. Some examples:

d21) 7...♘b4 8 ♗b1 ♗a6 9 ♘f3 ♕c7 10 ♘c3 e6 11 a3 ♘c6 12 ♗g5 left White with the better game in Schmittdiel-Grooten, Wijk aan Zee 1993 – he can't castle just yet, but the rest of his position is perfect.

d22) 7...e5 8 d5 (otherwise Black might play this move himself, as in the game I mentioned at the start: 8 a3 d5! 9 0-0 exd4 10 ♖e1 ♗e7 11 e5?! ♘xe5 12 ♗b5+ ♘fd7 13 ♘xd4 0-0 and Black had a solid extra pawn in M.Anderton-Collins, British Ch, Edinburgh 2003) 8...♘b4 9 ♗b1 ♗c5 10 0-0 a5 11 ♘b3 d6 (11...♗f8 12 h3 a4 13 ♘d2 b5 14 ♘c3 ♕a5 15 ♕e2 ♗c5 16 a3 ♘a6 17 ♘xb5 and White was a pawn up for nothing in Baklan-Zeller, Schwäbisch Gmünd 2000) 12 ♘g3 ♗c8 13 ♘xc5 bxc5 14 f4 ♕b6 15 fxe5 c4+ 16 ♔h1 ♘g4 was played in Van Beers-Kanep, European Team Ch, Plovdiv 2003. Here White missed the terrific shot 17 ♖xf7!! ♘f2+ (17...♔xf7 18 e6+ and 19 ♕xg4 gives White a decisive initiative, since Black's position is cut in two) 18 ♖xf2 ♕xf2 19 e6! (establishing a pawn-wedge right in the middle of Black's game) 19...0-0 20 a3 ♘d3 21 ♗xd3 cxd3 22 ♗d2 with superb compensation for the exchange – the bishop will dominate the long diagonal from c3, while a knight on f5 won't be tolerable for long.

5 ♘e2

A conservative development, though White retains the option of a later f4.

The immediate 5 f4!? is a little more bloodthirsty: 5...cxd4 6 ♘f3! (6 cxd4 f5 looks fine for Black) 6...dxc3 7 ♘xc3 with interesting compensation. I'd be quite happy with the white pieces in a practical game – try sorting out Black's development with a FIDE time-limit.

5...♗g7 *(D)*

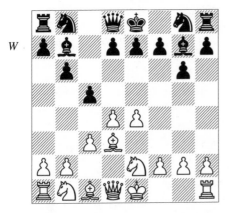

6 ♗e3

This is very compact. Defensively, the bishop guards d4, while White also has the option of ♕d2 and ♗h6 to exchange the g7-bishop.

6 ♗g5 is more active, but leaves White with some problems defending the d-pawn.

6...♘f6

As always in these 2...b6 lines, Black isn't worried about the white pawn advancing to e5, since this makes the b7-bishop into a much better piece.

7 ♘d2

The white minor pieces create a funny impression. Personally, I don't think that White can count on a real advantage with such a formation; his aggressive options are just too limited. 7 f3 is an interesting alternative, intending to exchange the g7-bishop with ♕d2 followed by ♗h6.

7...d6

7...♘g4 8 ♗f4 is no inconvenience to White.

8 h3 *(D)*

Cutting out any ...♘g4 ideas and preparing a later g4.

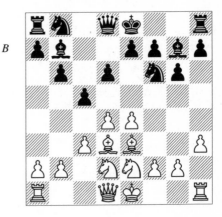

8...0-0

In such provocative systems, Black often delays or dispenses with castling, but here he can put the king into relative safety because White is not positioned to attack on the kingside. Even arranging the exchange of the g7-bishop, which is a crucial step in attacking a fianchetto, is problematic.

9 0-0

Similarly, White sees no value in playing on the h-file with h4-h5, and instead brings his rook to the f-file where it supports, and will benefit from, a quick run by the f-pawn.

9...♘bd7

White still has more space, but both black bishops are well placed, while White's cluster of minor pieces doesn't seem particularly active.

9...♘c6 is less logical, since the knight gets in the b7-bishop's way and is liable to be kicked by d5.

10 f4! *(D)*

Starting the most natural plan.

10...♖c8

Black develops his last queenside piece. Now play down the c-file is an option, while ...♖c7 and ...♕a8 (to exert pressure on the e4-pawn) is far from unprecedented.

11 a4

White decides to gain some queenside space too. This is always an option in such positions,

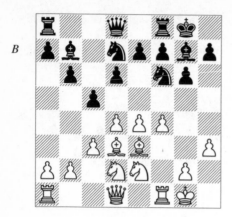

B

and I'm not sure whether it's a good or a bad idea. Certainly, such pawn advances weaken squares and increase the risk of over-extension, but the aggressive prospects they bring should not be underestimated. Instead, 11 f5 c4 12 ♗c2 e6 looks comfortable for Black.

11...a6!

This is a crucial concept in these restrained double-fianchetto positions – Black has to meet a4 with ...a6 (and h4 with ...h6) so that he can keep files closed: a5 will now be met by ...b5. Conceding space is a much riskier enterprise when you also allow lines to be opened.

12 g4

White has seized space across the board, and demands an accurate response of Black.

12...cxd4 13 cxd4 *(D)*

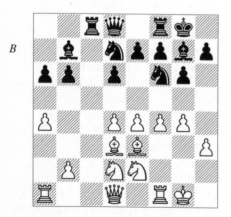

B

13...e5!

Staking a central claim at just the right moment. The white knights are ill-suited to cope

with this central break – they'd much rather be on c3 and f3.

I don't like 13...d5 as much, since after 14 e5 ♘e4 the g7-bishop is bottled up and White can break with f5 at will; e.g., 15 f5 gxf5 (15...♔h8 16 fxg6 fxg6 17 ♘f4 is also very strong for White) 16 gxf5 ♔h8 17 ♘f4 with advantage.

14 fxe5

Opening the f-file for the rook and the c1-h6 diagonal for the bishop is often a good idea, though the clearing of the d6-pawn gives Black some options too.

In view of the regrouping undertaken by Black on move 16, there's some merit in the idea of sidelining the f6-knight first, viz. 14 g5 ♘h5 15 fxe5 dxe5 16 d5, though ...♘f4 will be on the cards for some time.

Keeping the tension with 14 b4 is also worthwhile.

14...dxe5 15 d5

Both black bishops are now cut out, at least temporarily, but the black knights have been given excellent squares.

15...♘c5 16 ♗c2 *(D)*

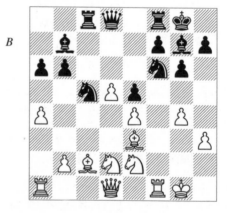

B

16...♘e8!

The knight aims for d6, where it is perfectly placed to block the d-pawn, hit the c4-square and prepare ...f5. 16...a5 is a decent alternative, entrenching the position of the c5-knight, but Postny makes the interesting decision to provoke b4, which will weaken White's control of c3 and c4.

17 ♘g3 ♘d6 18 b4

Taking the bait, as I would have done.

18...♘d7

White has a space advantage in all sectors of the board, but Black's pieces have a lot of potential, and he has no cause for complaint here.

19 ♘f3 ♘c4 20 ♗g5 (D)

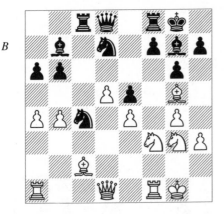

20...♗f6

20...f6 looks OK as well, and is a more ambitious way to play. The problem with this isn't the entombment of the g7-bishop (it was passive anyway) but the slight weakening of the a2-g8 diagonal and, more importantly, that now Black must be prepared for g5 by White, trying to weaken the black structure.

21 ♗h6 ♗g7 22 ♗g5 ♗f6 23 ♗h6 ♕e7!? *(D)*

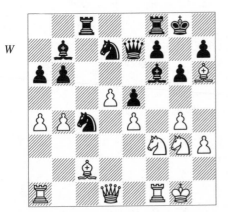

A fascinating attempt to keep the game alive.

24 ♕e1

24 ♗xf8 ♕xf8 leaves Black threatening both ...♘e3 and ...♕xb4 – the former would regain his lost exchange, while the latter would leave interesting positional compensation – two bishops, dark-square domination and a pawn in a position which isn't rook-friendly (not too many open files).

24...♗g7 25 ♗g5 ♗f6 26 ♗h6 ♖fe8 27 ♗d3 ♗g7 28 ♗g5 ♗f6 29 ♗h6 ♗g7 30 ♗g5 ♗f6 31 ♗c1 *(D)*

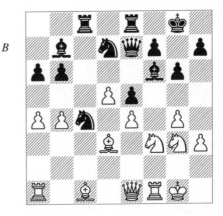

Now Erenburg plays the macho move. In any event, the players agree the inevitable draw in a couple of moves.

31...a5 32 b5 ♕b4 33 ♖a2 ½-½

It's unclear how either side can make progress. This was a hard-fought and instructive GM encounter.

Conclusions

1) Most of the sidelines covered here are perfectly playable. The reason they aren't more popular is that they don't place much pressure on the white centre.

2) 2...b6 is a good way to keep the game complex. 2...e5 is a solid defence, which resembles the Open Games.

3) Postny's double-fianchetto idea is interesting, non-theoretical and underused.

Index of Variations

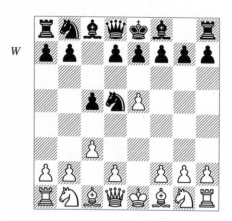

List of Games

Understanding the Chess Openings
Sam Collins
This indispensable one-volume reference work surveys all important chess openings. All main lines are covered, with typical strategies for both sides explained.
224 pages, 248 x 172 mm; $28.95 / £16.99

Chess Explained: The Classical Sicilian
Alex Yermolinsky
Former US Champion Yermolinsky explains the key plans and ideas of one of his preferred openings. This dynamic Sicilian variation has been a favourite of players such as Anand, Kramnik and Shirov.
112 pages, 248 x 172 mm; $19.95 / £12.99

How to Beat 1 d4
James Rizzitano
A repertoire for Black based on the counterpunching Queen's Gambit Accepted. Rizzitano also covers lines where White sidesteps the gambit.
160 pages, 248 x 172 mm; $27.50 / £15.99

Play the Open Games as Black
John Emms
Emms shows precisely how to deal with the Scotch, King's Gambit, Italian Game, Four Knights, etc.
224 pages, 210 x 145 mm; $23.95 / £15.99

Mastering the Chess Openings Volume 1
John Watson
In this massive tome focusing on king's pawn openings, Watson presents an holistic approach to understanding chess openings. He shows how an appreciation of ideas from one opening can lead to a greater understanding of other openings, and of the game as a whole.
336 pages, 248 x 172 mm; $29.95 / £19.99

The Ruy Lopez: A Guide for Black
Sverre Johnsen & Leif Johannessen
Provides Black with a complete repertoire with this most respectable of openings, together with a mass of insights and practical advice.
208 pages, 248 x 172 mm; $28.95 / £16.99

Chess Explained: The Queen's Indian
Peter Wells
An opening rich in nuances. Many of the modern main lines involve moves that look extravagant, but are backed up by a deep underlying logic.
128 pages, 248 x 172 mm; $19.95 / £12.99

Chess Explained: The English Opening
Zenon Franco
Grandmaster Franco explains the workings of this vast opening complex. He identifies the most distinctive and instructive lines, and illustrates them with outstanding modern examples.
112 pages, 248 x 172 mm; $19.95 / £12.99

How to Build Your Chess Opening Repertoire
Steve Giddins
Whether a novice or a master, every player needs to select an opening repertoire. The common-sense guidance includes advice on how to avoid being 'move-ordered'.
144 pages, 210 x 145 mm; $19.95 / £13.99

Creative Chess Opening Preparation
Viacheslav Eingorn
Grandmaster Eingorn is an chess opening trend-setter. Here he reveals the methods by which he prepares his openings, and shows the reader how new systems can be pioneered from scratch.
160 pages, 248 x 172 mm; $26.95 / £15.99

About the Publisher: Gambit chess opening books are designed to be different. We recruit the finest authors, writing on their specialist systems. Our editorial team is obsessive about double-checking variations and transpositions. We believe trustworthy analysis is important, and that an openings book can remain an asset over many years.

www.gambitbooks.com